Teacher Resource **Pack** for
OCR Psychology
AS Level

Fiona Lintern

Hodder Arnold

A MEMBER OF THE HODDER HEADLINE GROUP

Orders: please contact Bookpoint Ltd, 130 Milton Park, Abingdon, Oxon OX14 4SB. Telephone: (44) 01235 827720.
Fax: (44) 01235 400454. Lines are open from 9.00 – 6.00, Monday to Saturday, with a 24 hour message answering service. You can also order through our website www.hoddereducation.co.uk.

British Library Cataloguing in Publication Data
A catalogue record for this title is available from the British Library

ISBN-10: 0 340 87241 1
ISBN-13: 978 0 340 87241 3

First Published 2003
Impression number   10 9 8 7 6 5 4 3 2
Year   2007 2006 2005

Typeset by Fakenham Photosetting.
Printed in Great Britain for Hodder and Stoughton Educational, a division of Hodder Headline Plc, 338 Euston Road, London NW1 3BH by Hobbs The Printers Ltd, Totton, Hampshire.

For Alan, without whom this would never have been finished and for Sam, without whom it would have been finished a lot sooner!

Contents

INTRODUCTION   **1**

THE COGNITIVE APPROACH   **32**

Loftus and Palmer   32

Deregowski   40

Baron-Cohen, Leslie and Frith   47

Gardner and Gardner   55

THE DEVELOPMENTAL APPROACH   **61**

Samuel and Bryant   61

Bandura, Ross and Ross   66

Hodges and Tizard   73

Freud   78

THE PHYSIOLOGICAL APPROACH   **83**

Schachter and Singer   83

Dement and Kleitman   90

Sperry   95

Raine, Buchsbaum and LaCasse   99

THE SOCIAL APPROACH   **104**

Milgram   104

Haney, Banks and Zimbardo   110

Piliavin, Rodin and Piliavin   116

Tajfel   120

THE PSYCHOLOGY OF INDIVIDUAL DIFFERENCES   126

Gould   126

Hraba and Grant   131

Rosenhan   136

Thigpen and Cleckley   142

REVISING THE CORE STUDIES   150

Revision activities   155

Mark schemes   167

Psychological investigations   179

ACTIVITIES & EVALUATIONS   185

Introduction
Planning the course

The number of hours you have available per week and the number of weeks in the teaching year will vary from centre to centre. In an ideal environment, you would hope to have five hours a week for teaching AS Psychology but some centres allow only four hours and some teachers may be delivering the course in three hours or less at evening class. Some centres will have more weeks available to them in total, as teaching tends to start earlier in schools and sixth form colleges than in further education colleges. However many hours you have available, you should plan to cover one Core Study per week. Together with one week for each of the data collecting activities, this should leave you with approximately five weeks for revision.

You do have the option of **January examinations** and this decision will obviously affect your schemes of work. If you are keen to have students sit one unit in January, then Unit 2542 (Psychological Investigations) is probably the most appropriate. The four data collecting activities could be conducted before Christmas and students would have time to prepare for the examination over the holiday. Entering students for Units 2540 and / or 2541 in January is more complicated and if you are new to teaching it is probably best to plan for these examinations in the summer. However, those people teaching the whole A-level course in one year might find January examinations ideal.

You may share your teaching with another teacher and this will mean that the Core Studies and / or the data collecting activities will need to divided up between you. This is likely to mean that students are studying two Core Studies at the same time, but you can still use the same basic model of one Core Study in five (or four or three!) hours.

Assuming that you have five hours available to you, you could divide the time up as follows:

Hour 1: Background material
Hour 2 and 3: The Core Study
Hour 4: Evaluating the Core Study
Hour 5: Group Activities

This will obviously vary somewhat from Core Study to Core Study. Some require quite a lot of background material whilst others require very little at all. The method, procedure and results of some will take much longer than others and the evaluation may be more straightforward for some. You may also wish to allow time to show videos or to conduct mini-replications or role plays of some of the Core Studies. You may be able to cover the detail in the Core Study in one hour and make two hours available for group activities and so on. The five hour plan above does not include any preparation work done by the student prior to lessons and you may wish to set group or individual activities around researching background material or even reading, summarising and presenting the Core Study to the rest of the class. Students could complete summary sheets, evaluation sheets or short answer questions (see Study Guide for OCR Psychology) for homework. The ideas for group activities provided in this pack could also be used as homework exercises.

On the following pages are outline schemes of work, showing how you might cover everything in 30 weeks. This should allow for examination leave weeks, mock examinations, work experience and any other activities that prevent you from teaching! They are simply suggestions and there are many other ways of delivering the course, for example taking all the data collecting activities together at the start / end of the course. Photocopying to A3 should give you room to write notes on resources, homeworks etc.

Scheme 1 shows the straightforward scheme of work for one teacher planning to enter the students for all their examinations in the summer.
Scheme 2 shows a slightly modified version of this for one teacher planning to enter the students for Unit 2542 in January.
Scheme 3 shows a scheme of work for two teachers and summer examinations.
Scheme 4 is blank for your own planning.

ORDER OF STUDIES

There is no ideal order to deliver the course. For ease, I have kept the Core Studies and the data collecting activities in the order in which they appear on the specification but this is your choice. You should note however that questions on Unit 2540 appear in specification order.

I have advised in the teaching notes which accompany each Core Study (see later) that you choose relatively straightforward designs (such as Loftus and Palmer) to introduce the course but I have taught these studies in a variety of orders and have not experienced any problems.

ORDER OF DATA COLLECTING ACTIVITIES

Once again, there is no ideal order for these. The outline Schemes of Work keep them in order but in practice it may be best to link them with studies that use those data collecting techniques. For example, if you plan to conduct observations of animal behaviour it would make sense to have covered the Core Study by Gardner and Gardner immediately prior to this.

KEEPING STUDENT RECORDS

Following on from the Schemes of Work, there are some record keeping sheets: one for student details, one for attendance and one for keeping records of student work in relation to the Core Studies.

SCHEME 1

WEEK	CONTENT	RESOURCES/ ACTIVITIES	HOMEWORK
1	Induction activities		
2	Loftus and Palmer		
3	Deregowski		
4	Baron-Cohen, Leslie and Frith		
5	Gardner and Gardner		
6	ACTIVITY A		
7	Samuel and Bryant		
8	Bandura, Ross and Ross		
9	Hodges and Tizard		
10	Freud		
11	ACTIVITY B		
12	Schachter and Singer		
13	Dement and Kleitman		
14	Sperry		
15	Raine, Buchsbaum and LaCasse		
16	ACTIVITY C		
17	Milgram		
18	Haney, Banks and Zimbardo		
19	Piliavin, Rodin and Piliavin		
20	Tajfel		
21	ACTIVITY D		
22	Gould		
23	Hraba and Grant		
24	Rosenhan		
25	Thigpen and Cleckley		
26	REVISION ACTIVITIES		
27	REVISION ACTIVITIES		
28	REVISION ACTIVITIES		
29	REVISION ACTIVITIES		
30	REVISION ACTIVITIES		

SCHEME 2

WEEK	CONTENT	RESOURCES/ ACTIVITIES	HOMEWORK
1	Induction activities		
2	Loftus and Palmer		
3	Deregowski		
4	Baron-Cohen, Leslie and Frith		
5	Gardner and Gardner		
6	ACTIVITY A		
7	ACTIVITY B		
8	Samuel and Bryant		
9	Bandura, Ross and Ross		
10	Hodges and Tizard		
11	Freud		
12	ACTIVITY C		
13	ACTIVITY D		
14	Schachter and Singer		
15	Dement and Kleitman		
16	Sperry		
17	Raine, Buchsbaum and LaCasse		
18	Milgram		
19	Haney, Banks and Zimbardo		
20	Piliavin, Rodin and Piliavin		
21	Tajfel		
22	Gould		
23	Hraba and Grant		
24	Rosenhan		
25	Thigpen and Cleckley		
26	REVISION ACTIVITIES		
27	REVISION ACTIVITIES		
28	REVISION ACTIVITIES		
29	REVISION ACTIVITIES		
30	REVISION ACTIVITIES		

SCHEME 3

WEEK	CONTENT TEACHER 1	CONTENT TEACHER 2	RESOURCES/ ACTIVITIES	HOMEWORK
1	Induction activities	Induction activities		
2	Loftus and Palmer	Samuel and Bryant		
3				
4	Deregowski	Bandura, Ross and Ross		
5				
6	Baron-Cohen, Leslie and Frith	Hodges and Tizard		
7				
8	Gardner and Gardner	Freud		
9				
10	ACTIVITY A	ACTIVITY B		
11				
12	Schachter and Singer	Milgram		
13				
14	Dement and Kleitman	Haney, Banks and Zimbardo		
15				
16	Sperry	Piliavin, Rodin and Piliavin		
17				
18	Raine, Buchsbaum and LaCasse	Tajfel		
19				
20	ACTIVITY C	ACTIVITY D		
21				
22	Gould	Hraba and Grant		
23				
24	Rosenhan	Thigpen and Cleckley		
25	REVISION ACTIVITIES	REVISION ACTIVITIES		
26	REVISION ACTIVITIES	REVISION ACTIVITIES		
27	REVISION ACTIVITIES	REVISION ACTIVITIES		
28	REVISION ACTIVITIES	REVISION ACTIVITIES		
29	REVISION ACTIVITIES	REVISION ACTIVITIES		
30	REVISION ACTIVITIES	REVISION ACTIVITIES		

Variations

This assumes equal time for each teacher. You may need to share the studies out differently. You may want to cover one approach at a time (2 studies per teacher).
One teacher taking all the data collecting activities.

SCHEME 4

WEEK	CONTENT	RESOURCES/ ACTIVITIES	HOMEWORK
1			
2			
3			
4			
5			
6			
7			
8			
9			
10			
11			
12			
13			
14			
15			
16			
17			
18			
19			
20			
21			
22			
23			
24			
25			
26			
27			
28			
29			
30			

Psychology AS Student Information Form

Name:	Tutor:

Other subjects studied:	

Address:	GCSE results:
Phone number:	
Emergency contact number:	Previous school:

Details of text books issued:	Career aim (if known):

Any other information (special needs etc.):	

Predicted grade:	Actual grade:

Attendance register

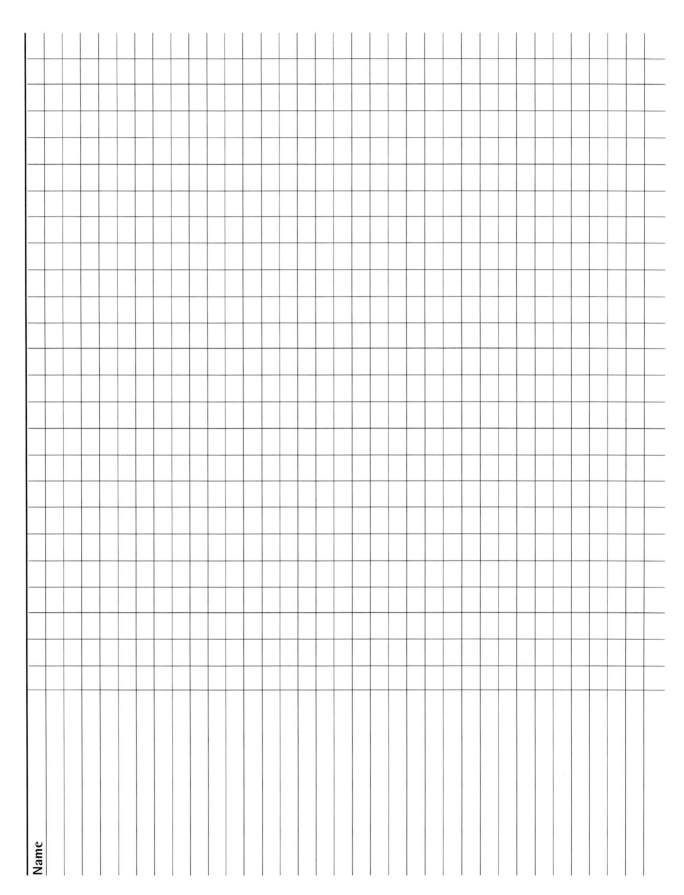

Name

Core Studies mark sheet

Name	1	2	3	4	5	6	7	8	9	10	11	12	13	14	15	16	17	18	19	20

OCR resources

OCR provides an 'e-list' where teachers of this specification can share ideas and ask questions. They also provide a website where users of the list can download resources supplied by other teachers. Contact the Subject Officer at OCR for more details.

Finally, OCR have a programme of INSET courses throughout the year in different locations. Your exams officer should have details of this programme and you can also check the OCR website at www.ocr.org.uk.

Resources

I would advise all new teachers to have a copy of the following texts:

Gross, Richard, **Key Studies in Psychology**. Hodder and Stoughton 4th edition 2003.

Banyard, Philip and Grayson, Andrew, **Introducing Psychological Research**. Palgrave 2000.

Oliver, Karon, **Psychology and Everyday Life**. Hodder and Stoughton 2000.

These three texts cover the Core Studies in varying amounts of detail. Gross gives complete versions of the studies, with detailed evaluation sections. The other two texts offer summaries of all 20 Core Studies with discussion. Oliver also includes extensive introductory material for each Core Study.

If you are planning to use either Oliver or Banyard and Grayson as the student text it would be advisable to have a copy of Gross for reference as it offers considerably more detail than the other two.

There is a Study Guide for students published in conjunction with this Teacher Resource Pack. The reference is Lintern, Fiona, **Study Guide for OCR Psychology**. Hodder and Stoughton 2003.

A good revision guide is Graeme Hill, **AS Psychology through diagrams**. Oxford Revision Guides 2001.

Philip Allan publish Student Unit Guides for **Core Studies 1 and 2** and for **Psychological Investigations**, which are inexpensive student purchases.

USING ORIGINAL ARTICLES

If your centre will pay for inter-library loans, or you have access to a university library, it would be a valuable resource to have a copy of each of the original articles. The specification does not imply that students should have read the original articles. You should note that the original reference for the Core Study by Freud is a book rather than an article and the summary in Gross is more than sufficient.

It is worth trying to get hold of these articles if you can, as each textbook varies in its coverage of the Core Studies and being able to check details in the originals is invaluable. Examiners use the content of original articles to set questions and not a specific book.

VIDEOS

Several companies now offer specially made videos for A-level Psychology. These cover a range of topics and are well worth investing in if your centre will provide some money.
Contact the following companies for their catalogues:

halovine video, 28 Ailsa Road, St Margarets, Twickenham, Middlesex TW1 1QW
Uniview Worldwide, PO Box 20, Hoylake, Wirral CH48 7HY
Resources in Training & Education (RITE), Cross Tree, Walton Street, Walton-in-Gordano, Clevedon, Somerset BS21 7AW

INTERNET RESOURCES

There are numerous internet resources for this specification. A search using any of the authors' names will identify their home pages and a wealth of further information. A complete list of websites is given in the Study Guide which accompanies this Teacher Resource Pack.

RESEARCH METHODS

Choose one of the research questions below and consider how psychologists might investigate this question:

- DOES VIOLENCE ON TV HAVE ANY INFLUENCE ON CHILDREN'S BEHAVIOUR?

- IS EYE WITNESS TESTIMONY ACCURATE?

- DOES NOISE AFFECT YOUR ABILITY TO DO HOMEWORK?

Address the following points in your discussion:

- How could you measure the *concepts (variables)* mentioned in the question?

- What would be an appropriate *sample* to use?

- What *resources* will you need?

- What *method* will you use?

- What *problems* might you encounter?

- Would anybody *object* to what you propose to do?

- What *type of information* will you collect in your investigation?

- What will you be able to do with this information?

Prepare an OHP to present to the rest of the class!

INTRODUCTORY EXERCISE: TRUE OR FALSE?

In groups, discuss whether you think each of these statements is TRUE or FALSE.
Why do you think this?
How could you test these statements?

Eyewitness testimony is usually accurate.

It is easy to make someone do something they don't want to.

Violence on TV encourages people to behave more violently.

It will never be possible to eradicate prejudice completely.

Everybody dreams every night.

AS Psychology course outline

UNIT 2540: CORE STUDIES 1 tests your knowledge of the following 20 studies and the way they were conducted.
UNIT 2541: CORE STUDIES 2 tests your ability to discuss and apply the issues raised by these 20 studies to a number of themes and debates.

THE COGNITIVE APPROACH

Loftus, E.F. and Palmer, J.C. (1974) Reconstruction of automobile destruction: an example of the interaction between language and memory. *Journal of Verbal Learning and Verbal Behaviour*, 13, 585–589.

Deregowski, J.B. (1972) Pictorial perception and culture. *Scientific American*, 227, 82–88.

Baron-Cohen, S., Leslie, A.M. and Frith, U. (1985) Does the autistic child have a 'theory of mind'? *Cognition*, 21, 37–46.

Gardner, R.A. and Gardner, B.T. (1969) Teaching sign language to a chimpanzee. *Science*, 165, 664–672.

THE DEVELOPMENTAL APPROACH

Samuel, J. and Bryant, P. (1984) Asking only one question in the conservation experiment. *Journal of Child Psychology and Psychiatry*, 25, 315–318.

Bandura, A., Ross, D. and Ross, S.A. (1961) Transmission of aggression through imitation of aggressive models. *Journal of Abnormal and Social Psychology*, 63, 575–582.

Hodges, J. and Tizard, B. (1989b) Social and family relationships of ex-institutional adolescents. *Journal of Child Psychology and Psychiatry*, 30, 77–97.

Freud, S. (1909) Analysis of a phobia of a five-year-old boy. In the *Pelican Freud Library* (1977), Vol 8, Case Histories 1, pages 169–306.

THE PHYSIOLOGICAL APPROACH

Schachter, S. and Singer, J.E. (1962) Cognitive, social and physiological determinants of emotional state. *Psychological Review*, 69, 379–399.

Dement, W. and Kleitman, N. (1957) The relation of eye movements during sleep to dream activity: an objective method for the study of dreaming. *Journal of Experimental Psychology*, 53, 339–346.

Sperry, R.W. (1968) Hemisphere deconnection and unity in consciousness. *American Psychologist*, 23, 723–733.

Raine, A., Buchsbaum, M. and LaCasse, L. (1997) Brain abnormalities in murderers indicated by positron emission tomography. *Biological Psychiatry*, 42 (6), 495–508.

© Hodder & Stoughton 2003

THE SOCIAL APPROACH

Milgram, S. (1963) Behavioural study of obedience. *Journal of Abnormal and Social Psychology*, 67, 371–378.

Haney, C., Banks, W.C. and Zimbardo, P.G. (1973) A study of prisoners and guards in a simulated prison. *Naval Research Review*, 30, 4–17.

Piliavin, I.M., Rodin, J.A. and Piliavin, J. (1969) Good Samaritanism: an underground phenomenon? *Journal of Personality and Social Psychology*, 13, 289–299.

Tajfel, H. (1970) Experiments in intergroup discrimination. *Scientific American*, 223, 96–102.

THE PSYCHOLOGY OF INDIVIDUAL DIFFERENCES

Gould, S.J. (1982) A nation of morons. *New Scientist* (6 May 1982), 349–352.

Hraba, J. and Grant, G. (1970) Black is beautiful: a re-examination of racial preference and identification. *Journal of Personality and Social Psychology*, 16, 398–402.

Rosenhan, D.L. (1973) On being sane in insane places. *Science*, 179, 250–258.

Thigpen, C.H. and Cleckley, H. (1954) A case of multiple personality. *Journal of Abnormal and Social Psychology*, 49, 135–151.

UNIT 2542: PSYCHOLOGICAL INVESTIGATIONS

This unit gives you the opportunity to try some of the methods that psychologists use. You will keep a brief record of the activities in a 'practical notebook' which you can refer to in the examination.

You will carry out FOUR data collecting activities (mini-investigations) during the year. These are:

● questions / self reports

● observations

● comparison of two conditions (experiment)

● correlation

BOOKS (for you to fill in)

Studying the Core Studies: some helpful hints!

In the examination you will be expected to demonstrate two skills:

- Your KNOWLEDGE and UNDERSTANDING of the studies.

- Your ability to EVALUATE and DISCUSS the studies in relation to a number of themes and issues.

Try to read the study before we start looking at it in class. This will give you a head start in identifying key issues. You will have a worksheet to complete on each study which will cover all of the important points. You will also have a piece of homework to complete when we have finished looking at each study. It would be very helpful to produce a summary of the key points and the key issues for revision purposes. The notes below will help you read, understand and make notes on the studies.

You should make notes on the following aspects of each study:

KNOWLEDGE AND UNDERSTANDING

- AIM
- METHOD(S)
- SAMPLE
- PROCEDURE
- RESULTS
- CONCLUSIONS

DISCUSSION AND EVALUATION

Evaluation is not difficult! It means providing a commentary on what you have learned. This might include all or some of the points listed below. You do not have to be an expert on psychology to evaluate a study – just think about the following points in relation to each study. All the terms below will be explained and discussed throughout the course. We will return to all of the studies at the end of the course and consider some of the wider themes and issues then.

- What STRENGTHS and WEAKNESSES of the way the study was conducted can you think of? (Each method has strengths and weaknesses which we will examine throughout the course.)

- How REALISTIC was the study? (Psychologists call this 'ecological validity'.)

- Was there any BIAS (for example in measuring behaviour, selecting samples etc.)?

- Were there any features of the study that might have given the participants 'clues' as to how to behave? (Psychologists call these 'demand characteristics'.)

- Are there any ETHICAL concerns with the study? Did participants consent to the study? Were participants deceived or distressed?

- How USEFUL was the research? What practical applications might it have?

Remember – your evaluation may differ from someone else's evaluation.
This is fine – but be prepared to justify your opinion!

STUDYING THE CORE STUDIES: SOME HELPFUL HINTS!

In the examination you will be expected to demonstrate two skills:

- Your KNOWLEDGE and UNDERSTANDING of the studies.

- Your ability to EVALUATE and DISCUSS the studies in relation to a number of themes and issues.

KNOWLEDGE AND UNDERSTANDING

- AIM

- METHOD(S)

- SAMPLE

- PROCEDURE

- RESULTS

- CONCLUSIONS

DISCUSSION AND EVALUATION

- What STRENGTHS and WEAKNESSES of the way the study was conducted can you think of?

- How REALISTIC was the study? (Psychologists call this 'ecological validity'.)

- Was there any BIAS (for example in measuring behaviour, selecting samples etc.)?

- Were there any features of the study that might have given the participants 'clues' as to how to behave? (Psychologists call these 'demand characteristics'.)

- Are there any ETHICAL concerns with the study? Did participants consent to the study? Were participants deceived or distressed?

- How USEFUL was the research? What practical applications might it have?

Making notes on a Core Study

1. AIM

In your own words, briefly explain the aim of the study.
What was the hypothesis (if there was one)?

2. METHOD

What type of design was used for this study (experimental, observational etc.)?
Why do you think that the researchers chose this design?
What advantages does this design have?
What disadvantages does this design have?
What were the variables?
How were the variables operationalised?
What controls (if any) were used?

3. SAMPLE

What was the target population in this study?
What was the sample size?
What type of sampling was used?
Does this type of sampling have any disadvantages?

4. RESULTS

Briefly say what the results of this study were.
Do the results support the hypothesis?
How were the results analysed?

5. CONCLUSIONS

What conclusions were drawn from this study?
What implications/applications are there from the findings of this study?

6. CRITICISMS

Does the study have any limitations (e.g. in terms of the method used or in terms of applying the results)?
Can you think of any ethical problems with this study?

SUMMARY SHEET

TITLE:

AUTHOR:

KEY WORDS:

AIM:

SAMPLE:

METHOD:

RESULTS:

CONCLUSIONS:

ISSUES/IMPLICATIONS:

Methodological issues	Themes
Sampling	Application to everyday life
Ecological validity	Determinism
Generalisation	Ethnocentrism
Ethics	Individual/situational explanations
Strengths and weaknesses of method	Nature–nurture
Qualitative and quantitative measures	Reductionism
Psychometrics	Usefulness
Reliability and validity	Social control

Study:

Choose THREE issues / themes and comment briefly on the named Core Study in relation to each issue / theme.

Issue / theme 1:

Issue / theme 2:

Issue / theme 3:

Example

Study:

Loftus and Palmer

Eye Witness Testimony

Issue / theme 1: SAMPLING

The sample were all students and so this might not be a very representative sample. Students may be different from other types of sample as they are younger, more used to remembering material, more likely to be affected by demand characteristics if they are receiving course credits for participation. May be non-drivers or less experienced drivers.

Samples also very small – study 19 ps in each condition.

Issue / theme 2: ECOLOGICAL VALIDITY

The event (car crash) was on video. There are several differences between video and real life: fewer emotional responses, expecting something to happen, paying attention, no consequences, knowing you are in an experiment etc.

Issue / theme 3: USEFULNESS

This study has several useful applications. It highlights the powerful effect of leading questions and this might have applications for the way that police / court etc. question people who are witnesses.

APPLICATION OF PSYCHOLOGY TO EVERYDAY LIFE

This refers to the extent to which we can explain **everyday behaviours** using the results of the core studies. What practical applications might each study have?

DETERMINISM

This is the argument that our behaviour is **determined** by factors outside our control. Behaviour may be determined by **biological factors** such as genes or hormones or by **situational factors** such as the reinforcements that we receive from others. The opposite argument is the **free will** argument which states that individuals are free to choose how to behave. Most psychological research is deterministic as it is trying to identify the factors or variables that determine behaviour.

ECOLOGICAL VALIDITY

If a piece of research is high in ecological validity it is easy to relate to real life. For example, an experiment conducted in very **realistic conditions** would be said to be high in ecological validity and an experiment conducted in very artificial conditions would be said to be low in ecological validity.

ETHICS

The British Psychological Society issues **ethical guidelines** for those engaged in psychological research. These guidelines are basically a set of rules outlining what is **acceptable** and what is not acceptable in research. For example, participants in psychological research should give their informed consent before the research starts, should not be deceived or distressed in any way and should have the right to withdraw from the research made clear to them.

ETHNOCENTRIC BIAS

This is defined as the tendency to interpret human behaviour from the viewpoint of our **own ethnic, social or other group**. This can lead to serious problems of 'scientific racism'. The term ethnocentrism is also used to refer to the tendency to **favour** our own group over others.

INDIVIDUAL AND SITUATIONAL EXPLANATIONS

This refers to the explanations of behaviour offered by the studies. An **individual** explanation would be **something about the person** (they fell over because they are clumsy) and a situational explanation would be **something about the situation** (they fell over because the floor was slippery). Some research suggests individual explanations of behaviour and some suggests situational explanations.

NATURE AND NURTURE

This is a very important debate in psychology and concerns the relative influences of inheritance and experience. *Nature* refers to the inherited or genetic make up of a person and *nurture* refers to all other influences from the moment of conception. Some of the core studies suggest the influence of inheritance and others suggest the influence of experience. As with many of these debates, some research suggests an **interaction between the two**.

PSYCHOMETRICS

Psychometric tests measure 'mental' characteristics. These include intelligence and personality and also aptitudes for certain jobs, and tendencies towards anti-social behaviours.

QUALITATIVE AND QUANTITATIVE MEASURES

Quantitative measures are numbers. Much research records behaviour in quantitative ways, for example by counting the number of aggressive acts or by asking people to rate their own behaviours or feelings on numerical scales. Qualitative measures do not use numbers and rely more on descriptions and interpretations of behaviour. Some research simply describes the behaviour of some individuals and an alternative to a numerical rating scale would be a more open-ended question where people simply describe how they feel.

REDUCTIONISM

This is the way in which psychologists often explain complex psychological phenomena by reducing them to a much simpler level, often focusing on a single factor. Most research is reductionist to an extent, as most experimental studies choose to examine the influence of single factors on complex behaviours.

REINFORCEMENT

A reinforcer is something that increases the likelihood of a behaviour occurring again. This may be in the form of a pleasant consequence such as praise or may be the avoidance of unpleasant experiences. This concept comes from learning theories in psychology and many behaviours can be explained as the result of learning.

RELIABILITY

Another word for reliability is **consistency**. If a measure is reliable it will give you consistent results. For example, a reliable psychometric test will give you the same (or similar) results if you test the same person on more than one occasion and a reliable observation schedule will mean that two or more observers will record the same results when observing the same behaviours.

VALIDITY

Does a measure actually measure what it claims to be measuring? Does a test of intelligence really measure intelligence or some other factor?

SOCIAL CONTROL

This concept refers to the attempt to use the results of psychological research to influence the behaviour of people. Some of the Core Studies have results which have been or could be applied in this way.

USEFULNESS OF PSYCHOLOGICAL RESEARCH

This refers to the extent to which psychological research can be used to improve something. This has obvious overlaps with Application of Psychology to everyday life and it is worth considering the uses to which the findings from each Core Study might be put.

Methods used by psychologists

EXPERIMENTAL METHODS

All experimental methods involve the manipulation of an INDEPENDENT VARIABLE (IV) and the CONTROL of all other variables. This means that the effect of changing the IV can be assessed (measured) in terms of change in the DEPENDENT VARIABLE. In other words, this allows us to test CAUSE and EFFECT relationships.

LABORATORY EXPERIMENTS

In the laboratory the experimenter deliberately manipulates the independent variable (IV) and maintains strict control over all other variables. See the Core Studies by Loftus and Palmer (eye witness testimony) and Bandura, Ross and Ross (imitation of aggression) as examples of laboratory experiments.

Strengths	Weaknesses
Manipulation of IV indicates cause and effect relationships	Total control over all variables is not possible
Increased control and accurate measurement	Artificial conditions may produce unnatural behaviour that lacks ecological validity
Standardised procedures = replication is possible	Results likely to be biased by sampling, demand characteristics, experimenter expectancy
	May raise ethical problems of deception etc.

FIELD EXPERIMENTS

Field experiments are carried out in a natural environment but the IV is still manipulated by the experimenter. See the Core Study by Piliavin, Rodin and Piliavin (Subway Samaritan) as an example.

Strengths	Weaknesses
Greater ecological validity	Difficulty in controlling the situation therefore more bias from extraneous variables
Less likelihood of demand characteristics (if people are unaware of study)	Difficult to replicate
	Time consuming
	Ethical problems of consent, deception, invasion of privacy etc.

NATURAL EXPERIMENTS

These take place in circumstances which allow the researcher to examine the effect of a naturally occurring independent variable (often used where artificial manipulation would be impossible or unethical). Quasi-experiments are any experiments where control is lacking over the IV. The Core Study by Hodges and Tizard (social relationships) does not manipulate a variable but examines its effects. The Core Study by Sperry (split-brains) also examines a 'naturally occurring' IV.

Strengths	Weaknesses
Greater ecological validity – since the change in the IV is a natural one	Difficult to infer cause and effect due to lack of control over extraneous variables and no manipulation of IV
If subjects are unaware of being studied there will be very little bias from demand characteristics	Impossible to replicate exactly
Allows researchers to investigate areas that would otherwise be unavailable to them	May be subject to bias if participants know they are being studied
Increased validity of findings due to lack of experimenter manipulation	Ethical problems of consent, deception, invasion of privacy etc.

OBSERVATIONAL METHODS

Psychologists often simply observe behaviour in real life situations without manipulation of the IV. Observations involve the precise measurement of behaviour in an objective way.

NATURALISTIC OBSERVATION

Naturalistic observation involves the recording of spontaneously occurring behaviour in the subject's own environment.

Strengths	Weaknesses
High ecological validity (especially if observer is hidden)	Cannot infer cause and effect relationships between variables that are only observed and not manipulated
Can be used to generate ideas for or validate findings from experimental studies	Lack of control means replication difficult
Often the only practical or ethical method for certain research questions	Risks of observer bias
	Ethical problems of invasion of privacy

CONTROLLED OBSERVATION

Controlled observation involves the recording of spontaneously occurring behaviour but under conditions contrived by the examiner. The Core Study by Dement and Kleitman (dreaming) uses controlled observation.

Strengths	Weaknesses
More control than naturalistic observation	Low ecological validity
Can allow more accurate observations	Demand characteristics
Greater control = easier replication	Behaviour may be unnatural if aware of being observed
Avoids problems of consent, deception etc. (unless observer and research purpose are hidden from participants)	Cause and effect cannot be inferred

PARTICIPANT OBSERVATION

Participant observations involve the researcher being involved in the everyday life of the subjects, either with or without their knowledge. The Core Study by Rosenhan (sane in insane places) is an example of participant observation.

Strengths	Weaknesses
Very high ecological validity if researcher 'undisclosed'	Difficult to record data promptly and objectively
	Impossible to replicate
Very detailed and in-depth knowledge can be gained	Researcher's presence may change situation or behaviour of subjects
Researcher gains 'first-hand' knowledge (not 'second-hand' as with surveys etc.)	Ethical problems, especially deception, consent and confidentiality
	Cause and effect cannot be inferred

Techniques similar to observation also exist for the observation of material such as television programmes or newspaper reports (content analysis) and for the observation of speech (discourse analysis).

QUESTIONING PEOPLE

There are many techniques for gathering self report data. These range from the superficial survey of many people to the in-depth assessment of individuals.

INTERVIEWS

All interviews involve direct (face to face) questioning of the participant by the researcher but they differ in how structured the questions are. Generally the advantages are that they produce a great deal of useful data (especially about internal mental states / beliefs / opinions) but a disadvantage is that relying on self report methods may not be reliable.

STRUCTURED INTERVIEWS
Contain fixed questions and structured ways of replying (yes / no etc.). The Core Study by Hodges and Tizard (social relationships) used interviews with adolescents and their parents.

Strengths	Weaknesses
Easy to quantify and analyse	Data may be distorted due to restricted answers
Reliable, replicable and generalisable	Some important information may be missed

SEMI-STRUCTURED INTERVIEWS
Contain guidelines for questions to be asked, but phrasing etc. are left up to the interviewer and some questions may be open-ended. Clinical interviews are 'semi-structured' (e.g. used in therapeutic contexts and by Piaget to explore children's cognitive development).

Strengths	Weaknesses
Fairly flexible and sensitive	Less reliable – open to experimenter bias
Fairly reliable and easy to analyse	Data is harder to analyse
	Difficult to replicate

UNSTRUCTURED INTERVIEWS
May contain a topic area for discussion but no fixed questions or ways of answering the questions. The interviewer is able to ask for clarification or explore answers in more detail.

Strengths	Weaknesses
Data is highly detailed and valid	No standardisation – so less reliable
Very flexible and unconstrained	Difficult to replicate and difficult to generalise
	Difficult to analyse

QUESTIONNAIRES

Questionnaires are written methods of gaining data from participants. They do not necessarily require the presence of a researcher. They include attitude scales and opinion surveys and may involve closed or open-ended questions.

Strengths	Weaknesses
Large amounts of data can be collected relatively quickly and cheaply, which increases representativeness and generalisability Replicable Closed questions are easy to score / analyse statistically	Lack flexibility Based on self report Social desirability bias, acquiescence, response set Very low response rate to postal questionnaires

Questionnaires also include PSYCHOMETRIC TESTS such as personality and IQ tests which, when standardised, are easy to administer and score, and allow us to make comparisons between individuals, especially in applied settings. However, it is difficult to construct reliable and valid tests. Some psychometric tests such as projective tests are much more subjective.

CORRELATION

Correlation is a method of data analysis used when we want to test for an association between two variables (unlike an experiment, when we are usually testing for a difference between two conditions). A positive correlation means that as one variable increases so does the other, and a negative correlation means that as one variable increases the other decreases. This does not tell you that there is a cause and effect relationship between these two variables, only that there is some form of relationship between them. Correlational data may be plotted on a scattergram and analysed using statistical techniques to give a correlation coefficient.

Strengths	Weaknesses
Gives precise information on the degree of relationship between variables No manipulation of behaviour is required so can be used in situations where experimentation would be impossible or unethical In some cases, strong significant correlations can suggest ideas for experimental studies to determine cause and effect relationships	No cause and effect can be inferred Correlation coefficients may miss interesting patterns in data Technique is subject to any problems associated with the method used to collect data

CASE STUDIES

Long term and detailed study of an individual or particular group. The case study method is often applied to unusual examples of behaviour which may provide important insights into psychological theories. The Core Studies by Freud (Little Hans) and Thigpen and Cleckley (multiple personality) are examples of case studies.

Strengths	Weaknesses
Produce highly detailed and in-depth data which other methods might miss	No cause and effect relationships can be inferred
Often the only suitable (or possible) method for studying some forms of behaviour	Cannot be generalised to wider population
Particularly appropriate for the study of 'exceptional' cases	Low reliability due to many case studies being retrospective (memory distortion)
	Questioning may produce demand characteristics
	Researcher may demonstrate bias
	Impossible to replicate
	Expensive and time consuming

REVIEW ARTICLES

Such articles are produced when researchers do not obtain their own data (primary data) but instead read and review a great many studies already published and draw general conclusions from them. See the article by Deregowski for an example of this.

Strengths	Weaknesses
Large amounts of data can be examined	Studies being reviewed may be flawed
Brings research together often for the first time – increases knowledge	Reviewer may be biased
Easier to access than many original papers	Difficult to ensure that a representative sample of all the relevant literature is reviewed

Ethical guidelines for research with human participants

GENERAL

Investigators must consider the **ethical implications and psychological consequences** for the participants in their research. Threats to their psychological well-being, health, values or dignity should be eliminated.

CONSENT

Whenever possible the investigator should **inform** all participants of the objectives of the investigation.

Research with **children** or with participants who have **impairments** that will limit understanding and / or communication (such that they are unable to give their real consent) requires special safeguarding procedures.

When research involves any person **under 16** years of age, consent should be obtained from parents or from those *in loco parentis*.

Investigators should realise that they are often in a position of **authority or influence** over participants who may be their students, employees or clients. This relationship must not be allowed to pressurise the participants to take part in, or remain in, an investigation.

The **payment** of participants must be not be used to induce them to risk harm beyond that which they risk without payment in their normal lifestyle.

DECEPTION

The **withholding** of information or the **misleading** of participants is unacceptable if the participants are typically likely to object or show unease once debriefed.

Participants should never be deliberately misled without **extremely strong** scientific or medical **justification**.

DEBRIEFING

Debriefing does **not provide a justification** for unethical aspects of any investigation. Some effects which may be produced by an experiment will not be negated by this process. Investigators have to ensure that participants receive any necessary debriefing in the form of active intervention before they leave the research setting.

WITHDRAWAL from the investigation

At the onset of the investigation, investigators should make plain to participants their **right to withdraw** from the research at any time, irrespective of whether or not payment or any other inducement has been offered.

CONFIDENTIALITY

Information obtained about a participant during an investigation is **confidential** unless otherwise agreed in advance.

PROTECTION of participants

Investigators have a responsibility to protect participants from **physical and mental harm**. Where research may involve behaviour or experiences that participants may regard as personal and private, the participants must be protected from stress by all appropriate measures, including the assurance that answers to personal questions need not be given.

In research involving children, **caution** should be exercised when discussing the results with parents, teachers etc.

OBSERVATIONAL Research

Unless those observed give their consent to being observed, observational research is only acceptable in situations where those observed could **expect** to be observed by strangers.

The cognitive approach
Loftus and Palmer

TEACHING NOTES

In order to teach this study well it is not necessary to give students a complete set of notes on memory first. This is a straightforward study which most students should grasp with very little background material.

This makes an ideal **first study** to teach as it is a relatively simple laboratory study and allows you to illustrate concepts such as **hypothesis, independent** and **dependent variable** and **control** in a simple context. This study also highlights issues such as **sampling, demand characteristics** and **ecological validity** in ways that are relatively easy for students to understand.

You could start by showing students a clip of an event such as a robbery or a relatively minor act of violence (for ethical reasons) and ask them to free recall. This could lead to a discussion of how accurate memories are. In my experience, most students will state that memory is accurate before doing this study! If you find that there is a variation in recall of detail you could ask students to generate a list of factors that might contribute to the accuracy of memory (note – you will get lots of non-psychological suggestions which might generate an interesting discussion about which ones psychologists might be interested in). You are looking for the suggestion **leading questions** to give you a nice 'way in' to this study.

Alternatively, show students a video clip and give them some questions to answer in the style of this study. This would demonstrate the effect of leading questions more explicitly but you may not have the opportunity for such a wide ranging discussion as simply asking for free recall.

Once you have set the scene you might also like to look at why the effect of leading questions might be an important one. The way police question suspects is an obvious application but your students may be able to come up with some more.

Next you could ask them to **design** a way of testing how leading questions affect memory. In my experience, students can do this quite well without the need for lengthy lectures on research methods first. The chances are that some will suggest 'real life' scenarios or set ups and you could introduce the notion of control here.

Now you can begin to outline the study. Encourage students to take notes about the aim, method, results and conclusions or use the worksheet supplied in this pack straight away.

STUDY 1

A very straightforward example of a laboratory study. Encourage the class to think about the **variables** and perhaps to write out an **experimental** and **null hypothesis** for this study. The researchers varied the verb used but they kept a number of other factors **constant**. Ask students to identify what these might have been; they include: the same questions with the exception of the critical one, the same film, the same environment for viewing, the same time period between seeing film and answering questions etc. Ask them to suggest reasons why the results showed a difference between the groups before giving them Loftus and Palmer's suggestions.

STUDY 2

This is very similar. Again students can be asked to identify the variables and write a hypothesis. In this study there is a **control group** who were not asked the critical question. You could ask students to suggest reasons why it is good idea to have a control group in psychological research.

DISCUSSION

The terms used in the study are complex but basically Loftus and Palmer are suggesting that either we give particular answers because we think we should (demand characteristics) or because the question has somehow affected our actual memory. Study 2 suggests that the second explanation can be supported.

Loftus, E.F. and Palmer, J.C. (1974)

Reconstruction of automobile destruction: an example of the interaction between language and memory. *Journal of Verbal Learning and Verbal Behaviour*, 13, 585–589

STUDY 1

In your own words, explain the *AIM* of this study.

The independent variable (IV) is the one that the experimenters manipulate and the dependent variable (DV) is the one that the experimenters measure.

Complete the following table:

Independent variable	Dependent variable

How many conditions of the IV were there? List them.

What did the experimenters control in this study?

What was the critical question?

Explain why the researchers asked several other questions even though they were only interested in the answer to one question.

Complete the following results table: What conclusions can you draw from these results?

Condition (verb)	Mean estimate
Smashed	
Collided	
Bumped	
Hit	
Contacted	

STUDY 2

In your own words, what was the *AIM* of the second study?

Complete the following table for the second study:

Independent variable	Dependent variable

In this study there were three conditions: 'hit', 'smashed', and a **control** group. Explain why researchers often use a control group in their studies.

What was the critical question in this study?

Complete the following results table (N is shorthand for number of participants):

Condition	N	Yes to critical Q	No to critical Q
SMASHED			
HIT			
Control			

What conclusions can you draw from these results?

Read the discussion of this article again. Loftus and Palmer offer two possible explanations for their findings. Explain what is meant by:

a) Distortion

b) Response bias

Give some examples of 'leading questions' in everyday life and suggest how they might influence our responses. Which explanation (distortion or response bias) is the more likely for each of your examples?

STUDY 1

Independent variable

VERB USED IN QUESTION

smashed / collided / bumped /

hit / contacted

Dependent variable

ESTIMATE OF SPEED

miles per hour

Condition (verb)	Mean estimate
Smashed	40.3
Collided	39.3
Bumped	38.1
Hit	34.0
Contacted	31.8

STUDY 2

Independent variable

VERB USED IN QUESTION

smashed / hit / control

Dependent variable

RESPONSE TO QUESTION:

DID YOU SEE ANY BROKEN GLASS? (yes / no)

Condition	N	Yes to critical Q	No to critical Q
Smashed	50	16	34
Hit	50	7	43
Control	50	6	44

IDEAS FOR GROUP / INDIVIDUAL ACTIVITIES

● Produce an EVALUATION of this study.

You could ask students to discuss the following points: how *realistic* the study was (think about the differences between these tasks and real life situations where you might need to remember what you had seen; this is referred to as the ecological validity of a study), who the *participants* were and whether the results could be generalised to other people, the *usefulness* of the research and so on.

Students should cover some or all of the following points in their discussion:

Realism/ecological validity: ecological validity was low; this was a laboratory study and the participants knew that it was an experiment. Real situations would have an element of surprise: you wouldn't be paying attention; there would be increased emotional content; there may be victims; you may not be asked questions till some time later; you may have discussed what you saw with people and so on.

Participants: the participants were all students. There are several ways in which students may not be representative of the general population: these might include age, educational experiences (used to paying attention and being tested?), driving experience, etc.

Usefulness: this study has many applications – police questioning people, teachers setting questions, etc.

Other issues might include the types of tasks – how easy is estimating speed? It may be easier for some groups than others (police officers or taxi drivers might be less affected by leading questions than students); the driver of the car is not mentioned in the article – what if they had been visible as an elderly woman or a young man? What if the car had been a Porsche or a SmartCar?

● **Make a list of all the factors that you can think of that might affect someone's memory of an event.**

You might like to begin by asking students to think about their own memory. If they had to give a account of what they were doing on a particular day, say 4 August last year, how accurate do they think their memory might be? What factors might affect this? Have they ever had the experience of recalling an event differently from a friend who was also there? What sort of differences were there in the memories? Where might these differences have come from?

There are probably dozens of answers to this! Some more obvious ones might include: time of day, eyesight, physical state (tired, drunk etc.), state of mind (preoccupied, worried, happy) and so on. Try to steer the students on to more psychological issues such as the following: type of event, complexity of event, stereotypes, expectations, previous experiences, personality, occupation, length of time between event and recall, type of questioning and so on. This might be a good exercise to do for just a few minutes or at the start of a lesson. (You could spend a long time on this without necessarily getting anything more useful than you can get in five minutes.)

● **Design a study investigating an aspect of EWT. What strengths and weaknesses does your study have?**

You could ask students to start by thinking about an appropriate **research method**. Loftus and Palmer used a laboratory experiment for their research and you may have already discussed the strengths and weaknesses of this method. How about suggesting the use of a field experiment or a case study? Ask students to work in groups and present their study to the rest of the class, identifying TWO strengths and TWO weaknesses with their design. Alternatively, if you only have a few minutes you could do this as a large group exercise at the end of a lesson.

This is a good introduction to research methods. If you haven't taught any research methods yet, you will find that students are still able to do this task although they may not have the correct terminology (field study etc.). The best strengths and weaknesses to concentrate on at this stage of the course are probably **ecological validity / realism** (a field study would have higher ecological validity than a laboratory experiment), issues relating to **control of extraneous variables** (easier in a laboratory experiment) or **demand characteristics** (if participants know they are in a study how will their responses be affected?).

Deregowski

TEACHING NOTES

This is a **review article** which examines research into the ways different cultures perceive pictures. It is important to explain to your students what a review article is. Reviews are written to summarise a body of research and to draw general conclusions about the area of research. They may also be written to evaluate previous research (see Gould for an example of this). Explaining that research is published in journals and that it is very useful for someone to review a body of knowledge is often helpful.

It is not necessary to give students a full introduction to theories of perception, although you may want to introduce the notion that **perception is an active process** rather than a passive one. You may also want to distinguish between the process of seeing (a physiological process) and the process of perceiving (a psychological process).

I usually introduce this using some pictures starting with the Necker Cube (see OHP). The Necker Cube is a two-dimensional representation of a three-dimensional object. We have learned to perceive such images in this way. Try to explain to your students that not everyone who looks at this picture will perceive it as three-dimensional. Any of the 'impossible figures' will also allow you to illustrate this. They exist (on paper) in two dimensions but could not exist in three dimensions even though this is what our brain is telling us should happen. This will allow you to introduce the notion of 'depth cues': the cues that we are familiar with that tell us that the image we are looking at is a representation of three dimensions (such as trees getting smaller as they get further away, nearer objects overlapping those further away and so on).

If you teach this study following on from Loftus and Palmer, you could use a very similar introductory exercise. Rather than asking students for factors that influence memory, this time you can ask them for factors that influence perception. You will probably get a similar list of factors and many may be non-psychological again, but you should steer students in the direction of **learning, prior experiences and expectations**. This can also be illustrated by reference to visual illusions (the B / 13 illusion, the ambiguous figures and so on). Focus on perception of pictures (try drawing a very similar perspective picture such as a road going into the distance with trees on either side and ask students how they interpret this).

You are looking to focus in on **culture** (or learning) as one variable that affects perception of pictures. The notion that we learn to interpret pictures is quite a difficult one and you may want to look for some examples of cartoons, logos or other images that make a lot of assumptions about how people will interpret them. Many cartoon images use lines to represent movement, for example.

The other key issue related to this study is **ethnocentrism** but this is best left until you have discussed the study. Ethnocentrism is defined as the tendency to interpret all behaviours by the standards of your own culture (or the tendency to over-value your own group at the expense of others). This is illustrated in the anecdotal evidence quoted by Deregowski as well as the interpretation of 'two-dimensional perceivers' as somehow less able or less advanced. This is a good place to introduce these ideas and the notion of scientific racism. This topic is well covered by Banyard in *Controversies in Psychology* (1999, Chapter 4).

Deregowski, J.B. (1972)

Pictorial perception and culture. *Scientific American,* **227, 82–88.**

This is a *REVIEW ARTICLE*. Deregowski did not conduct the research reported here but has written a review of a number of pieces of research (mainly conducted by Hudson) on cultural differences in *perception of pictures*.

The question Deregowski poses at the start of the article is as follows:

'Do pictures offer us a lingua franca *for inter-cultural communication?'*

What does this question mean?

1   THE ANTELOPE / ELEPHANT PICTURES

Hudson suggests that South African Bantu workers had trouble interpreting *depth cues* in pictures. (Pictures are two-dimensional (flat) but depth cues allow us to represent the three-dimensional world in two-dimensional pictures.) Hudson's picture of the antelope and the elephant contains three depth cues.

Explain what each one is:

Familiar size:

Overlap:

Perspective:

Outline the *findings* of Hudson's research with these pictures.

2   THE IMPOSSIBLE TRIDENT

Look at the picture of the impossible trident for a few minutes. Cover this up and try to reproduce the picture here. If you get stuck have another look but do not start drawing again until you have covered up the picture!

Was that easy or difficult? Can you suggest reasons?

Whom did Hudson test using the trident figures?

How might the results of this study be explained?

3   SPLIT-STYLE DRAWINGS

What is a split-style drawing? Draw a split-style hamster!

What advantages do split-style drawings have over 'perspective' pictures?

CONCLUSION

Do pictures offer us a *'lingua franca* for inter-cultural communication'?

What does Deregowski conclude?

ETHNOCENTRISM

Explain what is meant by ethnocentrism.

Give examples of ethnocentrism from Deregowski's article.

Do pictures offer us a 'lingua franca' for inter-cultural communication?

HOW MANY DIMENSIONS
DOES THIS HAVE?

IDENTIFY THE DEPTH CUES
IN THIS PICTURE

IDEAS FOR GROUP / INDIVIDUAL ACTIVITIES

Ethnocentrism is defined as the tendency to see others from the perspective of our own group (racial, cultural, social). Try to identify some examples of ethnocentric statements or assumptions from Deregowski's article and then discuss the following questions:

What are the effects of making such statements?

Why should we regard ethnocentrism as a problem in Psychology?

Ethnocentrism is quite a difficult concept to grasp and there may be other studies that offer you a better opportunity to develop this idea (Tajfel, Hraba and Grant, Gould all relate to this issue). It may be enough here simply to ensure that students have identified the biases in this article, including:

● the **anecdotal evidence** which implies that other cultures are somehow less developed than Western culture because they fail to interpret the images that we are familiar with.

● the **assumptions** that Western styles of art / drawing are superior to other cultures.

More generally, **Western Psychology** dominates our psychological knowledge. If such research is done from an ethnocentric viewpoint then we are failing to include a large proportion of the world in Psychology. Further, we may be contributing to the reinforcement of prejudiced notions of other cultures and to the assumption that Western culture is the 'best'. Banyard identifies some of these problems in his book *Controversies in Psychology*. He states that contemporary Psychology texts often use terms such as **societies** when referring to the Western world and **tribes** when referring to other parts of the world (and to animals). Ask your students how they would feel if a psychologist wrote about natives or tribes when referring to them!

● **What problems do you think that researchers face when conducting (or even planning to conduct) cross-cultural research?**

This is a useful exercise to make time for. There are many problems that you can consider here, including the **time involved** and the difficulties in **funding** such research. There are also practical problems such as **language difficulties** and translation problems. There are also problems more directly related to the issue of ethnocentrism. You could argue that it is almost impossible for a researcher to lose all their own **cultural assumptions** and simply observe what is happening in another culture. Such research is clearly **socially sensitive** and raises several ethical issues.

TEACHING NOTES

It is well worth investing in some dolls that you can use to act out this study. If you can find a black doll and a white doll you can use them again for the study by Hraba and Grant. This Core Study does not have a complex procedure but students will follow the scenario better if you act it out for them – and they will find it amusing to see you playing with dolls!

Students will need a brief introduction to the nature of autism. You may wish to do this as a simple short lecture style class or if you have time this could be set as a piece of research. This is a very easy topic to research on the internet; the National Autistic Society has a website, for example, which clearly sets out the characteristics of childhood autism. Students could research this and produce a short description of autism or they could present their findings to the rest of the class. (There will be lots of opportunities to do this type of activity, so one group could do this task and another group the next research task etc.)

If you do this as a lecture style introduction, try to cover the following:

THE CHARACTERISTICS OF AUTISM

In particular, the 'triad' of impairments that are typically experienced by those with autism. These are:

IMPAIRED SOCIAL INTERACTION
Autistic people typically have difficulty with social relationships and often appear to be aloof and indifferent to other people.

IMPAIRED SOCIAL COMMUNICATION
Autistic people typically have difficulty with verbal and non-verbal communication and in particular do not understand the meanings of gestures, facial expressions or tone of voice. They will take everything that is said to them literally.

IMPAIRED IMAGINATION
Autistic children typically do not develop pretend play and other imaginative skills in the way that other children do. They may have a limited range of imaginative activities which may be copied and pursued rigidly and repetitively.

As well as this triad of impairments, autistic people tend to have repetitive behaviour patterns and are very resistant to changes in routine.

(Above information taken from the National Autistic Society website: www.nas.org.uk.)

THEORY OF MIND
Theory of mind is defined as the ability to **impute mental states to oneself and to others**. In other words, someone with a theory of mind recognises that others have minds (thoughts, knowledge and emotions) and will be able to understand that these may be different from their own. This ability to make inferences about what other people believe to be the case in a given situation allows one to predict what they will do. Lacking a theory of mind leads to difficulties in social relationships. Any form of pretend play is virtually impossible, understanding emotional responses

is very difficult indeed and so on. The lack of a theory of mind is one way in which the impairments described above have been explained.

Students often confuse theory of mind with egocentrism. Egocentrism is seeing the world from your own perspective and decentring is the ability to look at the world from another's perspective. This has obvious overlaps with the notion of theory of mind, but lacking a theory of mind is lacking the understanding that other people have minds. Baron-Cohen, Leslie and Frith use the phrase 'treat people and objects alike' in their article and this often helps students understand this notion.

You could ask students to come up with their own ideas about how you could test whether someone has a theory of mind or not, although this is quite a difficult task to do and you may find that they struggle with the answers. Some suggestions include: not understanding when someone is upset or happy or experiencing any type of emotion, any situation where an autistic person does not understand that someone has not heard or seen a piece of information, playing almost any game at all.

A NOTE ABOUT THE PARTICIPANTS

Students often focus on the different numbers of participants in each group as a problem. This is a good place to introduce the notion of 'natural' or 'quasi' experimental research. In such research the participants are not randomly or opportunistically selected participants assigned to different groups but are already existing groups of children with either Down's syndrome, autism or neither of these disorders. (Referring to this group as 'clinically normal' is probably better than simply 'normal' as this raises issues of labelling etc.)

Baron-Cohen, S., Leslie, A.M. and Frith, U. (1985)

Does the autistic child have a 'theory of mind'? *Cognition, 21, 37–46*

Briefly outline the *characteristics of AUTISM*.

What is meant by having a *theory of mind* (ToM)?

Why do we need a theory of mind?

What problems might be encountered by somebody *without* a theory of mind?

THE STUDY

To investigate whether or not someone can understand the notion that other people have beliefs, you can use tasks that require the participants to attribute a belief state to another person. The task used here is a 'false belief' task called the *Sally-Anne task*.

The researchers used three groups of children in a 'quasi-experimental' design. What is meant by this?

Complete the table below with the details of each group.

	N	Mean chronological age (CA)	Mean verbal mental age (vMA)
Autistic			
Down's syndrome			
Clinically normal			

Why do you think that the researchers used the group of Down's syndrome children in this study?

Outline (as briefly as you can) the Sally-Anne task.

The children were asked FOUR questions during the test. What were they?

NAMING QUESTION:

BELIEF QUESTION:

REALITY QUESTION:

MEMORY QUESTION:

The results table in the article gives the percentages of children in each group who answered the questions correctly. The naming, reality and memory questions were answered correctly by all the children.

Complete the following table showing the actual number (you have to convert from percentages) of children who answered the belief question correctly.

No. of children answering correctly	Autistic	Down's syndrome	Clinically normal
BELIEF QUESTION			

What conclusions can you draw from this?

In the results section, the researchers state that the difference between the autistic children and the other children is *statistically significant at the level of p < 001'*.

Explain what this means.

CRITERIA FOR CHILDHOOD AUTISM

THE TRIAD OF IMPAIRMENTS

IMPAIRED SOCIAL INTERACTION

Autistic people typically have difficulty with social relationships and often appear to be aloof and indifferent to other people.

IMPAIRED SOCIAL COMMUNICATION

Autistic people typically have difficulty with verbal and non-verbal communication and in particular do not understand the meanings of gestures, facial expressions or tone of voice. They will take everything that is said to them literally.

IMPAIRED IMAGINATION

Autistic children typically do not develop pretend play and other imaginative skills in the way that other children do. They may have a limited range of imaginative activities which may be copied and pursued rigidly and repetitively.

As well as this triad of impairments, autistic people tend to have repetitive behaviour patterns and be very resistant to routine.

(Above information taken from National Autistic Society website: www.nas.org.uk.)

THEORY OF MIND

Theory of mind is defined as:

the ability to **impute mental states to oneself and to others**.

In other words, someone with a theory of mind recognises that others have minds (thoughts, knowledge and emotions) and will be able to understand that these may be different from their own.

This ability to make inferences about what other people believe to be the case in a given situation allows one to predict what they will do.

	N	Mean Chronological Age (CA)	Mean verbal Mental Age (vMA)
Autistic	20	11 years 11 months	5 years 5 months
Down's syndrome	14	10 years 11 months	2 years 11 months
Clinically normal	27	4 years 5 months	assumed = to CA

No. of children answering correctly	Autistic	Down's syndrome	Clinically normal
BELIEF QUESTION	4	12	23

IDEAS FOR GROUP WORK / INDIVIDUAL ACTIVITIES

- ● What criticisms might be made of this study?

Some students might pick up on the **number of children** in each group. Although you could argue that the small numbers may make the samples lack representativeness the different numbers in each group are not in themselves a problem (see Teaching notes).

Students are also likely to suggest **task problems** and in particular the **use of dolls.** A good argument might be that it is inappropriate to ask an autistic child to attribute thought to a doll. Remember that autistic children do not have the skills required for pretend play. Would acting this out with real people be better? Leslie and Frith conducted further research to investigate this idea. They conducted the same experiment using real people rather than dolls and found the same results. This would suggest that the criticism that the use of dolls is a problem is unfounded. However, you could still suggest that the dolls might have been a less appropriate scenario for the older children (or for the boys). You could also set this group task as one which simply looks at the problems of using dolls in this study rather than problems generally.

- ● Design a test for theory of mind.

I have already said that this is quite a difficult task and the more you think about it, the more ingenious the Sally-Anne task appears. However, it is worth asking students to think about this. They may not find this a difficult task and may come up with some original suggestions; and even if they do struggle, they will have learned something about how difficult it is to test this notion. Some pointers might include: any task where a person needs to read facial expressions, interpret emotional responses or work out that someone else does not have access to all the same information.

Gardner and Gardner

TEACHING NOTES

This is the only animal study currently on the AS specification. You will probably need to touch on the relevance of animal studies to an understanding of human behaviour. However, I would not recommend that you spend too long on this as it cannot be asked specifically as a Core Studies 2 question as there are no other studies to tie in with it.

To give your teaching of this Core Study a focus I would suggest having two main questions to consider.

These are:

HOW WAS WASHOE TRAINED TO USE SIGN LANGUAGE?

The researchers used **shaping**, **imitation** and **reinforcement** to train Washoe and you will need to explain these terms to the students (see OHP).

HOW WAS HER LEARNING MEASURED?

The researchers chose an arbitrary form of measurement which was as follows: once a sign had appeared it was put on a list. It was recorded each day for 15 days. They found that 30 signs met these criteria (see OHP).

There have been many attempts to define criteria for language acquisition and these vary. For example, Aitchinson suggests 10 criteria for language, including semanticity, displacement and structure dependency and these are covered in the summary of the article by Banyard. Graeme Hill focuses on vocabulary, differentiation, transfer and combinations in his summary and Oliver discusses transfer, generalisation, differentiation and delayed imitation. These issues are not discussed by the Gardners in their article but it is a worthwhile exercise to consider one of these sets of criteria and ask students which ones they think that Washoe met.

This study is available on video and students always enjoy watching this. However, you need to be careful when showing it as some of the results are later ones than are given in the published article (number of signs learnt etc.). One video also includes a 'double blind' test of Washoe's learning which is not mentioned in the article. Students will need to focus on the information in the article for answering examination questions.

There are some excellent internet resources available for this study. Try www.cwu.edu/~cwuchci and search this site.

A NOTE ABOUT PSYCHOLOGICAL INVESTIGATIONS

Observational research can be conducted at your local zoo! Many zoos will provide talks about chimpanzee behaviour and may even have some ideas for observational studies. I have done this at Chester Zoo for the past three years and students have observed such behaviours as handedness, mother–infant interaction, time budgets and facial expressions. As well as being very enjoyable, it is an excellent introduction to observational methods and the students usually have few problems in evaluating their own research and suggesting improvements. Issues such as ecological validity and ethics are also well illustrated.

Gardner, R.A. and Gardner, B.T. (1969)

Teaching sign language to a chimpanzee. *Science,* 165, 664–672

This case study is one of the earliest attempts to teach a chimpanzee to use sign language. The issue of whether or not animals can use sign language has been a long-running debate in Psychology. Lenneberg, for example, argues that 'there is no evidence that any non-human form has the capacity to acquire even the most primitive stages of language development'. When he wrote this (in 1967) the Gardners had already started their research with Washoe. We will come back to this statement at the end of the study.

This research was a case study. Describe one strength and one weakness of the case study method.

Why did the Gardners not teach Washoe to speak?

What is ASL and why did the Gardners choose this to teach Washoe?

Explain the procedure followed by the researchers. In other words, how did the Gardners encourage Washoe to use sign language? (Try to use some or all of the following terms in your description: operant techniques, shaping, imitation.)

Explain how the researchers recorded Washoe's signs.

In some studies with Washoe, the researchers used *deaf* adults to record the signs. What advantages would this have?

After 22 months, how many signs did Washoe have? Give some examples of the signs she used.

There have been many attempts to define criteria for language – that is, a set of specified abilities that must be demonstrated before we conclude that Washoe really was using a language and had not simply learned some impressive tricks.

Identify TWO criteria which were satisfied by Washoe's signing and give evidence for these.

Identify TWO criteria which were NOT satisfied by Washoe's signing.

How does Washoe's language development compare to that of a child?

Outline the conclusions that can be drawn from this study. Do you *agree or disagree* with the statement made by Lenneberg at the start of this article?

'there is no evidence that any non-human form has the capacity to acquire even the most primitive stages of language development'

Lenneberg, 1967

'gimme-tickle'

Washoe, 1969

SIGNS USED BY WASHOE WITHIN 22 MONTHS OF THE BEGINNING OF TRAINING
(IN ORDER OF APPEARANCE)

1 come–gimme	Made to persons / animals and when objects were out of reach Combined: 'come-tickle', 'gimme-sweet'
2 more	Used for more food etc. and also for a repetition of activities such as swinging or tickling
3 up	To reach something, to sit on shoulders, to leave potty chair
4 sweet	Dessert or candy
5 open	House door, rooms, car door, fridge, cupboard, containers, taps
6 tickle	For tickling / chasing games
7 go	Indicating direction while walking / on someone's shoulders
8 out	Passing through doorways, asking to go out
9 hurry	Usually after 'come-gimme', 'out', 'open' and 'go', often used when waiting for food
10 hear–listen	For loud or strange sounds, bells, car horns, asking for a watch to be held to her ear
11 toothbrush	After a meal, or when shown a toothbrush
12 drink	Water, milk, soft drinks (combined with 'sweet')
13 hurt	To indicate cuts and bruises on herself or others; could be elicited by red stains on a person's skin or tears in clothing
14 sorry	After biting someone, or when someone had been hurt (not necessarily by Washoe), when told to apologise
15 funny	When soliciting play, during play, occasionally when being pursued, after doing something she shouldn't have done
16 please	When asking for objects and activities, combined with 'go', 'out' and 'drink'
17 food–eat	During meals and preparation of meals
18 flower	For flowers
19 cover–blanket	At bedtime or naptime, or when going out in the cold
20 *dog	For dogs and barking
21 you	To indicate turns in games or in response to questions such as 'who tickle?'
22 napkin / bib	For bib, washcloth and tissues
23 in	To go indoors / ask someone to come indoors
24 brush	For hairbrush or to ask for brushing
25 hat	For hats and caps
26 *I–me	Washoe's turn, when sharing items / food, in phrases 'I drink' or in response to questions such as 'who tickle?'
27 shoes	For shoes and boots
28 *smell	For scented objects, tobacco, perfume, sage etc.
29 pants	For nappies, trousers etc.
30 clothes	For Washoe's jacket, nightgown, shirts and for other people's clothing
31 cat	For cats
32 key	For keys and locks / ask for a door to be unlocked
33 baby	For dolls, including toy horse and duck
34 *clean	Used when Washoe was washing or being washed, when someone else was washing hands or an object, also for soap

*These four signs did not meet the stringent criteria set by the researchers but were observed on more than half the days in a 30-day period. Strictly this means that **30 signs** were learned during the first 22 months.

IDEAS FOR GROUP / INDIVIDUAL ACTIVITIES

● **Do you think that this research was ethical?**

There are several issues which could be discussed here.

1   Washoe was bought from an animal importer. She would have been taken from her mother at a very young age (add details of maturity etc.) and brought to the United States.
2   She was cared for in isolation. She did not have the company of other chimpanzees until the study was over and she was moved to a primate research centre.
3   Use of animals for psychological research. This may turn into a big debate and you need to remember that this is now the only animal study on the specification. However, it is a worthwhile debate if you have the time, and students could research some of the organisations that are promoting 'human rights' for the great apes.

● You could ask students if they think that there might have been 'experimenter or observer bias' (the researchers seeing what they wanted to see) in this study. They could consider how such bias might be overcome.

● You could also take this opportunity to discuss the strengths and weaknesses of the case study method. As one of my students pointed out, Washoe could have been a very stupid chimp (or a very clever one) and the Gardners are trying to draw conclusions about *all* chimps from the study of Washoe.

● You could set a task involving internet resources. Using the search words 'Washoe' and 'chimpanzee' (to avoid all the references to Washoe county) generates an enormous number of useful sites. Washoe now lives at the Chimpanzee and Human Communication Institute (CHCI) and there are several sites linking you to a 'chimpcam' where you can view Washoe and the other signing chimps. One of these is Loulis, Washoe's adopted son who was taught sign language by Washoe. There is also an organisation called Friends of Washoe (www.friendsofwashoe.org) and this website has many links to organisations promoting the rights of the great apes and campaigns to prevent these animals being used in research.

The developmental approach
Samuel and Bryant

TEACHING NOTES

You will need to give students some background material on Piaget's theory for them to understand this Core Study. However, it is worth keeping this as short as possible. Giving them too much may lead to them confusing other studies with the one that they need to know for the examination.

A video would be a good way to introduce this study – the one produced by Uniview (see **Resources**, page 11) includes an outline of Piaget's theory with some of the major evaluation issues and shows many of the classic studies being conducted. It also contains a very brief account of theory of mind and the Core Study by Baron-Cohen, Leslie and Frith (autism).

SOME OF THE KEY ISSUES TO COVER INCLUDE

- It is important that students understand the nature of Piaget's theory: that it is a **stage theory** that proposes that children are capable of performing **different kinds of cognitive 'operations' at different ages.**

- It is also important that students understand the definition of **conservation** – you could easily act this out for them!

- Finally they need to understand why Samuel and Bryant felt that it was necessary to **replicate the original Piagetian study and how they changed this.**

The results can appear confusing at first. There are lots of them and the figures given are the **mean number of errors made**. As each child was tested four times on each of the mass, number and volume tasks they could make a maximum of 12 errors.

Make sure that students understand that some of the evidence **supports Piaget** (certain tasks are easier than others, conservation skills increase with age) and some evidence does **not support** Piaget (asking two questions confuses children as when they are tested only once they make fewer errors). Use the table in the worksheet to summarise these points.

PSYCHOLOGICAL INVESTIGATIONS

OCR generally dissuades people from using participants under 16 years for experimental work. However, why not see what conservation skills students over 16 have?

The fixed-array condition is an interesting one – could you judge whether there was the same amount in two containers if you had not seen the liquid poured into them from equivalent original containers? You could choose some familiar containers (litre bottles of fizzy drinks, litre cartons of milk and litre cartons of fruit juice often look very different) and this could be the basis of a practical experiment.

Samuel, J. and Bryant, P. (1984)

Asking only one question in the conservation experiment. *Journal of Child Psychology and Psychiatry*, 25, 315–318

We have looked briefly at the research conducted by Piaget and his theory of cognitive development. The study by Samuel and Bryant *replicates* one of Piaget's studies with a crucial change.

Describe the *typical Piagetian task* to test for conservation of *volume* (you might find it easier to draw pictures to help you remember!).

Outline Samuel and Bryant's *criticism* of this.

Write a *hypothesis* for this study and identify the *independent and dependent variables*.

Describe the THREE conditions of this experiment.

Standard	
One judgement	
Fixed–array	

This experiment used *independent measures*. What does this term mean?

The researchers also used THREE types of task with each child. These were conservation of mass (plasticine), conservation of number (counters) and conservation of volume (beakers of water). Each child was tested four times on each task – giving a total of 12 trials for each child.

Complete the results table below.

AGE	Experimental condition		
	Standard	One judgement	Fixed-array
5 years			
6 years			
7 years			
8 years			

NB – numbers in article are MEAN errors on all tests (maximum = 12, minimum = 0)

Do these results *support* Samuel and Bryant's hypothesis? Explain your answer.

What does this table tell you about the effect of AGE on ability to conserve?

The article also suggests that ability to conserve depends on the *type of conservation task* (mass, number and volume). Which task did the children find the easiest and which the most difficult?

This study offers both support for and criticisms of Piaget's original work. Summarise these in the table below:

Support for Piaget	Criticisms of Piaget

MEAN NUMBER OF ERRORS IN EACH CONDITION

AGE	Experimental condition		
	Standard	One judgement	Fixed-array
5 years	8.5	7.3	8.6
6 years	5.7	4.3	6.4
7 years	3.2	2.6	4.9
8 years	1.7	1.3	3.3

IDEAS FOR GROUP / INDIVIDUAL ACTIVITIES

- A researcher wishes to conduct a piece of research using children from a local school. Write a short 'advice sheet' for them covering practical issues, methodological issues and ethical issues.

There are several studies in this specification that involve the use of children. These are Baron-Cohen, Leslie and Frith, Samuel and Bryant, Bandura, Ross and Ross, Freud, Hodges and Tizard, Tajfel, Hraba and Grant. It is worth getting your students to consider the issues surrounding research with children even though they are not allowed to conduct this sort of research themselves for their Practical Work Folder.

These issues might include:

PRACTICAL / METHODOLOGICAL ISSUES

Use of language, type of task appropriate for age, children's attention span, children's interest / motivation, leading questions.

ETHICAL ISSUES

Parental consent, protection, allowing children to withdraw if they appear to be distressed.

- Design a study which would investigate the one-question / two-question variable but in another context (not conservation skills). Identify the strengths and weaknesses of your study.

Samuel and Bryant's study has many implications. One of these relates to the questioning of children in general and may have overlaps with the issue of leading questions considered in the Core Study by Loftus and Palmer. If children are witnesses and are questioned, will they change their answer if asked the same question twice, which would inevitably happen in this kind of situation? It should be relatively straightforward for students to design a study that investigates this question.

Bandura, Ross and Ross

TEACHING NOTES

You may wish to take the opportunity provided by this Core Study to introduce theories of learning, although the basic idea in this study of **learning by imitation** should be easy for students to understand without a lot of background theory. If you do have time to consider learning as a more general topic you could cover the concepts of instrumental (operant) conditioning and classical conditioning. The only other Core Study with direct discussion of conditioning is Gardner and Gardner. However, the concepts may be useful in explaining the results of several other studies (Tajfel, Hraba and Grant and perhaps even Haney, Banks and Zimbardo, Milgram and Rosenhan could be explained in terms of learned responses). Chapter 14 in *Key Studies in Psychology* (Gross, 2003) deals with theories of learning and *Psychology and Everyday Life* (Oliver, 2000) has a whole section on theories of learning, with some excellent examples.

You could introduce this study by asking students for a number of suggestions as to why children might be aggressive. They will undoubtedly offer the suggestions that you are looking for (because they copy it, from others, from television etc.) and this will introduce the idea of being able to investigate this hypothesis experimentally. Students will also voice their concerns about the ethical implications of conducting such research and it is probably best to acknowledge their comments and return to the ethical debate after the study (see Ideas for individual / group activities).

This is a familiar study to most teachers although the details of the study are perhaps more complex than are reported in most introductory textbooks.

There are several **hypotheses** being tested:

- that observing aggression will lead children to display more aggressive behaviour

- that children will be more likely to imitate same sex role models

- that boys will generally show more aggressive behaviour than girls (this last one could lead into a discussion of the nature–nurture debate: discussing whether boys are more aggressive than girls for biological or social reasons, and this could take you back to a discussion of theories of learning).

The children were **matched** on 'pre-existing levels of aggression' before the study began and this was rated by the experimenter and by a teacher in the university nursery where the children attended. Children were rated on four 5-point scales measuring physical aggression, verbal aggression, aggression towards inanimate objects and aggressive inhibition (described as the tendency to inhibit aggressive reactions in the face of provocation and deemed to be a measure of aggression anxiety). Inter-rater reliability (measured by Pearson's product moment) was .89. Children were then arranged in groups of three and assigned to either the aggressive model condition, the non-aggressive model condition or the control condition. Although students do not have to know this much detail about the studies, it might be worth mentioning this part of this particular study as it would allow you to discuss issues related to observation (observer bias, inter-rater reliability) and the reasons for matching participants in experimental research.

There are also some complex forms of **measurement** in this Core Study which may need some consideration. As well as recording (by observation through one-way mirrors) imitative physical and verbal aggression, the observers also recorded instances of mallet aggression, punching the Bobo doll (which the aggressive model did not do), other acts of aggression that were not imitative, and aggressive gun play.

There are many **ethical** issues to cover in your discussion of the study (see Ideas for group / individual activities for more detail) including the lack of consent from parents, the distress caused to children, the fact that they were prevented from playing with attractive toys and the fact that the experimenters set out to induce aggression in the children.

This study has many **implications**, most notably the effects of watching aggression on television and perhaps playing aggressive video games. Whilst not specifically relevant to the study, there are issues of **practical applications** and **usefulness** to deal with for Core Studies 2 and you may wish to mention the coursework assignment for A2 at some point during the AS course. It is likely that students will find articles that relate aggression to the playing of video games etc.

PSYCHOLOGICAL INVESTIGATIONS

It would obviously be unacceptable to conduct any research that attempted to manipulate a negative variable such as aggression. However, it would be possible to conduct questionnaire research on the topic of attitudes to violence on television, or whether parents report that children *do* copy behaviours they see on television. It would also be possible to conduct a content analysis of children's television programmes as the observational activity. However, I would recommend trying to conduct observations of real life behaviour, if possible.

Bandura, A., Ross, D. and Ross, S.A. (1961)

Transmission of aggression through imitation of aggressive models. *Journal of Abnormal and Social Psychology, 63, 575–582*

What was the AIM of this study? What practical applications might there be for the results of this study?

Who were the participants in this study? (Note: there is no information relating to parental consent given in the article.)

Complete the table below with details of the experimental groups:

Group	No. of children	Sex of children	Sex of model	Aggressive / non–aggressive model
1				
2				
3				
4				
5				
6				
7				
8				
control				

What problems might there be with research conducted on groups of this size?

One way of reducing *subject variability* is to '*match*' the children. Matching means pre-testing on important variables and then ensuring that each group is made up of participants who are similar in their scores on these variables.

Explain how the children in this study were matched.

Observers rated the children on each of the four scales. What criticisms can you make of observer ratings?

Tests of *inter-rater reliability* found a *high positive correlation* between the ratings of two observers. Explain what the terms 'inter-rater reliability' and 'correlation' mean.

THE PROCEDURE

Briefly outline the three stages of the experimental procedure:

Stage 1:

Stage 2:

Stage 3:

The observers recorded THREE measures of imitation. What were these?

1

2

3

What else did they record?

Summarise the results in point form (you do not need to know all the numbers!).

Group	No. of children	Sex of children	Sex of model	Aggressive / non-aggressive model
1	6	M	M	A
2	6	M	M	N-A
3	6	M	F	A
4	6	M	F	N-A
5	6	F	M	A
6	6	F	M	N-A
7	6	F	F	A
8	6	F	F	N-A
control	(24)			

RESULTS:

Children in *aggressive model conditions* made more aggressive acts than children in non-aggressive model conditions.

Boys made more aggressive acts than girls.

Boys in *aggressive model conditions* made more aggressive acts when model was male.

The girls in the *aggressive model conditions* showed more physical aggression when the model was male but more verbal aggression when the model was female (but see 'punches Bobo' results).

MEASURE OF	RESPONSE
IMITATION	1 Imitative physical aggression
	2 Imitative verbal aggression
	3 Imitative non-aggressive verbal responses
INCOMPLETE IMITATION	1 Mallet aggression
	2 Sits on Bobo
NON-IMITATIVE AGGRESSION	1 Punches Bobo
	2 Non-imitative physical and verbal aggression
	3 Aggressive gun play

IDEAS FOR GROUP / INDIVIDUAL ACTIVITIES

● **What conclusions can be drawn from this study? Could you generalise the results of this study to the possible effects of viewing violence on television or playing violent computer games?**

This is an obvious implication of this research and in fact Bandura went on to test this idea by showing children films of the model in one of his later studies. This is worth spending some time on as this is a common issue for students to select in their A2 coursework assignment as well as being topical.

● **Consider the ethics of this study. Should it have been conducted? How could you overcome any ethical problems that you have identified?**

My personal opinion is that this Core Study is probably the most unethical of the 20 on the AS specification. There is no mention of parental consent. Children were rated for aggressiveness by teachers and experimenters. They were distressed by the model's behaviour and by not being allowed to play with toys. They were in strange rooms with unfamiliar people and so on. If you have mature students who are parents, ask them to imagine their children taking part in this research.

You could extend this activity by asking students to suggest how some of these problems might be overcome, but apart from asking for parental consent, the whole study would need redesigning to avoid breaking ethical guidelines.

● **Design a study to investigate the effects of TV violence. What problems might you encounter in conducting such research?**

If you have not done this as an introductory exercise you may want to do it now.

This is ideal for small groups who could present their ideas to the rest of the class along with the problems (practical, ethical) that would be encountered.

If you have time to spend on this, you could use this to explain why correlation is often used when experiments would be impractical or unethical and also why correlation is not causation because you have not manipulated any variables.

Hodges and Tizard

TEACHING NOTES

This Core Study is the only **longitudinal** study on the AS specification and so it is worth spending a few minutes explaining the purpose of longitudinal studies as well as their strengths and weaknesses. You could perhaps ask students to generate the strengths and weaknesses and also to think of some topic areas that might be best researched in this fashion.

There are two important areas to cover before you start looking at this Core Study.

1 **Theoretical background:** as with most of the Core Studies, students are not expected to know background theories / evidence for the examination. However, the topic of **attachment and maternal deprivation / privation** is well covered in all introductory textbooks and is an important area of psychological research. It is worth considering giving students a brief overview of some of the key ideas in this area, such as the work of Bowlby and Rutter or possibly some of the case studies of severe deprivation (see Banyard, *Introducing Psychological Research* for summaries of key research in this area). Alternatively, you could simply ask students to generate ideas about what exactly infants need for 'normal' social development.

2 **Previous reports on this longitudinal study:** earlier studies by Tizard and other researchers have reported on this same group of children throughout their lives, and this Core Study has a companion article (Hodges and Tizard (1989), IQ and behavioural adjustment of ex-institutional adolescents, *Journal of Child Psychology and Psychiatry*, 30, 53–75) which covers different aspects of the research conducted at age 16. Some of this material is covered in the Introduction to this study (see Gross, *Key Studies in Psychology*, pages 276–278) although you may wish to obtain a copy of this companion article.

This Core Study focuses on a fairly straightforward research question (what are the effects of early deprivation on later social relationships?) but includes a variety of measures and a huge number of results. If you have the original article or are working from Gross, you need to summarise these. There are **two important comparisons** to make:

● What are the differences between the ex-institutional children and the controls?

● What are the differences between the restored children and the adopted children?

You could make this more manageable for the students by asking them to draw up a chart comparing these groups.

Note: although this is a relatively straightforward study to teach, you may want to consider the needs of your individual students before you embark on it. If you know that anyone you teach has experienced any form of institutional care or has had a particularly disrupted childhood then this can become an extremely sensitive study to teach. I once taught this study to a group of mature students which included more than one student who had been in institutional care and several whose children were currently in care and they were hoping for them to be returned to them. If you are in this position, it might be wise to avoid some of the more emotive discussion topics or at least give students warning of the material that will be covered.

Hodges, J. and Tizard, B. (1989b)

Social and family relationships of ex-institutional adolescents. *Journal of Child Psychology and Psychiatry, 30, 77–97*

Hodges and Tizard's research is *longitudinal*. Explain what is meant by this term.

What are the *advantages* and *disadvantages* of longitudinal research?

The participants in this research spent the first two years of their lives in institutional care, before being either adopted or returned to their biological parents. They were followed up and assessed at various stages until the age of eight and were then re-assessed at the age of 16 for this study. A comparison group of children who had been with their biological families throughout their lives was also included in this study.

This makes the research '*quasi-experimental*'. Explain what is meant by this term.

When the participants were assessed at age 4, there had been 65 children. This study followed up 39 children. What term is given to this 'loss' of participants in longitudinal research?

Comparisons were made between THREE groups in this study. What were the groups?

Group 1	
Group 2	
Group 3	

FIVE principal methods of collecting data were used in this study. Summarise them in the table below:

1	
2	
3	
4	
5	

The original article has a huge results section suggesting many differences between the groups. The article summarises FIVE main findings between the ex-institutional groups and the comparison groups.

Summarise these in the table below:

1 |_____
2 |_____
3 |_____
4 |_____
5 |_____

Hodges and Tizard also report differences between the adopted children and the restored children. What were these differences and how do Hodges and Tizard explain them?

CONCLUSIONS

Outline one piece of evidence that suggests that the problems of disruption in early life *can* be overcome.

Outline one piece of evidence that suggests that the problems of disruption in early life *cannot* be overcome.

Can the differences observed between the ex-institutional groups and the comparison groups at age 16 definitely be put down to the early institutional experiences of the former?

FIVE METHODS OF COLLECTING DATA

- Interview with adolescent subject
- Interview with mother (and father)
- Self report questionnaire on 'social difficulties'
- Questionnaire for teachers on relationships with peers (and teachers)
- The Rutter B scale (standard psychiatric test).

FIVE KEY FINDINGS

THE EX-INSTITUTIONAL ADOLESCENTS

- Were more often 'adult-oriented'
- Were more likely to have 'problems getting on with peers'
- Were less likely to have a 'special friend'
- Were less likely to 'turn to peers for emotional support'
- Were less likely to 'be selective in choosing friends'.

IDEAS FOR GROUP / INDIVIDUAL ACTIVITIES

● Construct two tables, one comparing the ex-institutional children with their controls and a second comparing the adopted and the restored children. What conclusions can be drawn from these tables?

You may have done this as you were teaching the Core Study but it is worth spending some time looking at a summary of results and asking students to draw conclusions from them. There are different issues to consider with each comparison: the ex-institutional children generally have more problems with social relationships than their controls, but the adopted children seem to have fared better than those restored to their natural families. You could ask students to generate suggestions for explaining these differences.

● 'Mother love in infancy is as important for mental health as are vitamins and minerals for physical health' (Bowlby 1951). Does this study support this statement?

This is a classic quote from Bowlby's argument that bad homes are better than good institutions. This can make for a heated debate though, so as I have already suggested in the Teaching notes, you need to be aware of the personal circumstances of the students in your class before embarking on activities such as these.

● Select any one of the FIVE methods of data collection used in this study and write a short evaluation of it.

A good exercise with a big class, where you can give each group one of the methods to consider. This is good revision of the strengths and weaknesses of interview and questionnaire research as well as giving you the opportunity to talk about psychometric tests (Rutter B scale). This task also makes a good presentation exercise.

Freud

TEACHING NOTES

The first issue to consider here is how much material you wish to give the students. The reference for this Core Study is not a journal article but one of Freud's case histories and the case of Little Hans covers over 100 pages of this book. It is quite heavy reading and it is perfectly possible to teach this study without having read the original. The most detailed summary is in Gross and both Banyard and Oliver offer simple summaries of the major points.

You will obviously need to cover some background material, but not the entire case in detail. Not only is this likely to be very time consuming, but it may also have the unwanted effect of leaving the students believing that they need to know a great deal more information for the examination than they actually do.

You will probably need to spend an hour introducing Freud's theory and my suggestions would be to cover the following:

1   **A brief history:** who Freud was, his training as a doctor, his interest in 'hysterical' disorders and his proposals (radical at the time) that the mind could affect the body.
2   The development of **Freud's theories of psycho-sexual development**, and in particular the **Oedipus complex.** You could also cover Freud's tripartite structure of personality as the terms **id, ego** and **superego** are often familiar to students. If you focus on the Oedipus complex then you can set the Core Study in the context of Freud's claim that Hans was going through the Oedipus complex. **What evidence is there for this claim?** Freud claimed that Hans had a phobia of horses due to his fear of his father. **What evidence is there for this claim? What other explanations might there be?**
3   The **methods** used by Freud in his treatment. These are probably worth mentioning briefly. Although they are not all evident in this study, the general technique of **interpretation** is an important one for students to consider.

You may also want to touch on the following issues:

This is a **case study**. There are other case studies on the AS specification (Gardner and Gardner, Thigpen and Cleckley) and students should be able to describe the strengths and weaknesses of this approach. It may be worth ensuring that students can do this even if you have covered this elsewhere.

This is a study about a **child** and so some of the issues concerning research with children (see Samuel and Bryant) are also relevant here, such as use of language etc. You may also want to point out to students that this is one of the only case studies of a child that Freud conducted and it was mainly conducted by post. They should not need much help in evaluating that!

Freud, S. (1909)

Analysis of a phobia of a five-year-old boy. In the *Pelican Freud Library* (1977), Vol 8, Case Histories 1, pages 169–306

Freud offers this case study (along with many others) as support for his theories of unconscious determinism, psycho-sexual development, the Oedipus complex, phobias and psychoanalytic therapy.

The case study of Little Hans is one of the more unusual case studies. It is the only one of Freud's case studies dealing with a child and the therapy was conducted through correspondence with Han's father rather than with the child himself. Hans was three years old at the start of the study and six when Freud published the study.

Why did Hans's father contact Freud? What aspects of Hans's behaviour was he concerned about?

Hans was analysed and treated through his father (who was a firm believer in Freud's theory) based on his reports of Hans's behaviour and statements. Treatment was achieved through:

1 Inferring the unconscious causes of Hans's behaviour through interpretation and decoding of Freudian symbols.
2 Confronting Hans with the unconscious causes by revealing to him his hidden motivations and consciously discussing them.

How were the following incidents interpreted?

1 Fear of bath

2 Taking the small giraffe from the bigger one

3 Fear of being bitten by white horses

4 Fantasy of being father with his mother

Hans is reported as having 'a lively interest in his widdler'. Freud used this as evidence that Hans was in which stage of psycho-sexual development?

Explain what Freud meant by the 'Oedipus complex' (or conflict).

What evidence is there in this case study for the existence of the Oedipus complex?

Freud interpreted Hans's fear of horses as symbolic of his fear of his father. What *other explanation* might there be for this fear?

Read the following extract of conversation between Hans and his father:

> *Father: When the horse fell down did you think of your daddy?*
>
> *Hans: Perhaps. Yes. It's possible.*

Suggest one problem with this type of questioning.

What would have been a better question?

Do you think Hans was abnormal? Give reasons for your answer.

This was a *case study*. What are the advantages and disadvantages of case studies?

Incident	Interpretation
Fear of bath	Freud suggested that Hans was frightened that his mother didn't love him as much now that his little sister had been born. This is reflected in his fear that she would not hold on to him as tightly in the bath and might let him go under the water.
Taking the small giraffe from the bigger one	Taking his mother away from his father – offered as evidence for the existence of Oedipus complex. Hans wants his mother to himself.
Fear of being bitten by white horses	Freud suggested that the horses were a symbol for Hans's father – offered as evidence for the Oedipus complex. Hans is afraid that his father will punish him for his feelings.
Fantasy of being father with his mother	A classical Oedipal fantasy – note that Hans keeps his father in the picture as the grandfather. Wishing to usurp father's place in the family but perhaps afraid to fantasise about getting his father out of the way altogether.

IDEAS FOR GROUP / INDIVIDUAL ACTIVITIES

● Write an evaluation of Freud's methods of collecting data in this case.

This should be straightforward for students to do individually or in groups. They should cover the fact that Hans and Freud met only once, that the father communicated with Freud by letter, that the father was a big fan of Freudian theory and therefore biased in his presentation of the material, the leading questions used by the father and so on. You could also use this activity to ensure that students are able to describe the strengths and weaknesses of case studies in general.

● Freud claimed that you could not treat phobias directly as they are simply symptoms of deeper (unconscious) problems. Behaviourists disagree. Find out what is meant by a desensitisation hierarchy and design one for treating one of the following phobias:

spiders
public speaking
agoraphobia

This is a fun activity if you have some spare time. Behaviourist theory is only really touched upon in this specification (Gardner and Gardner, Bandura), yet it is an extremely important aspect of Psychology. Encouraging an understanding of these theories might help students explain some of the findings of other studies, particularly in the Social and Individual Differences sections. Students should be able to research these ideas easily and will enjoy drawing up desensitisation hierarchies. You could ask them to suggest how Hans's fear of horses would have been treated by a behaviourist.

The physiological approach
Schachter and Singer

TEACHING NOTES

Emotions have proved to be a very difficult area to research and it is probably true to say that we still have no clear definitions of exactly what an emotion is. Is it (simply) a subjective experience? Is it a set of physiological responses? Is it both and if so, how are these two things related? In other words, how are the physiological and the psychological aspects of emotion related to each other? Before you can consider this Core Study, you will need to introduce students to this debate.

The most straightforward way to introduce this study may be to look briefly at theories of emotion. You can do this as follows:

Put very simply, the **James–Lange** theory proposed that external stimuli cause specific physiological responses (such as adrenaline release and increased heart rate) and that this is 'felt' as emotion. In this theory the physiological response is both necessary and sufficient for the occurrence of an emotional state.

Also put very simply, the **Cannon–Bard** theory proposes that emotion eliciting external stimuli produces two separate reactions: firstly the thalamus sends signals to the hypothalamus to trigger the physiological responses and secondly the thalamus sends signals to the cortex. These signals are registered ('felt') as fear. In this theory the physiological response is neither necessary nor sufficient for the occurrence of emotion.

Both of these theories can be criticised: the James–Lange theory because it has been shown that physiological changes are not different for all emotions (although they are for the most basic ones, such as fear); also, when injected with adrenaline, not all subjects report feeling emotions. The Cannon–Bard theory can be criticised for assuming that physiological changes have no influence on emotion. There are several studies that indicate that this does have a role and that Cannon and Bard overestimated the role of the thalamus. Again, there are studies indicating important roles for other brain areas. Further, much of the evidence presented for this theory is based on animal research.

Schachter and Singer's **cognitive labelling theory** (or TWO-FACTOR theory) proposes that external stimuli cause general physiological responses and that these must be interpreted (cognitive appraisal) as a particular emotional feeling. In this theory, physiological arousal is necessary but is not sufficient for the experience of emotion as cognitive appraisal may label the same physiological arousal in a number of different ways.

(See Graeme Hill, *Advanced Psychology in Diagrams* for an excellent summary of these theories and of the Core Study.)

Schachter and Singer's experiment stands as a milestone in emotion research as it provides evidence for their two-factor theory. It is a difficult study to teach students as it is quite complex and there are lots of conditions. However, the basic ideas are not difficult and if you explain a little about the above theories first you should be able to summarise the key points from the study.

SOME KEY POINTS TO COVER INCLUDE

An explanation of the three propositions at the start of the study. The study really has one hypothesis: that general physiological arousal is interpreted on the basis of the context in which the arousal takes place. It may be enough to ensure that students understand this basic proposition as the three further propositions are really conclusions from this initial statement. Simply, they suggest that if we experience a general state of arousal, we will use the cognitions available to us to label this arousal; if we have a ready explanation (in this case having been injected with something and told of the likely effects), we will not need to use external cues to label the arousal as emotion. Finally, if we do not have physiological arousal, we will not experience any emotion even if there are available situational cues which we could use.

You may also need to explain that one of the experimental conditions is 'missing': the misinformed group were not tested with the angry stooge. This means that there are seven conditions in all. Schachter and Singer explain that they originally conceived of the misinformed group as a further control group and that its inclusion in the euphoria condition was enough.

PSYCHOLOGICAL INVESTIGATIONS

Emotion is measured in two ways in this Core Study: behavioural **observation** and **self report**. If you are planning your observational activity, this might give you a good opportunity to consider the types of categories that the researchers used to observe behaviours in the euphoria and anger conditions. Full details are given in the original article and in Gross (page 535). Even if you do not intend to do anything related to this study or have already conducted the observation, an evaluation of these observational categories would be a useful exercise.

Participants were also asked to rate their own emotions on seven-point scales. They rated how 'irritated, angry or annoyed' they felt and then they rated how 'good or happy' they felt. These questions were included in a questionnaire with several other questions relating to physical symptoms and other emotional experiences. The scores used in the results tables are **happiness minus anger**; in other words, the higher the positive value, the happier the participants rate themselves as feeling. This could also be used as an introduction to self report measures (perhaps for positive emotions you should avoid asking about negative experiences) or an evaluation exercise.

Schachter, S. and Singer, J.E. (1962)

Cognitive, social and physiological determinants of emotional state. *Psychological Review, 69, 379–399*

Schachter and Singer's TWO-FACTOR THEORY of emotion proposes that emotion comes from a combination of:

_____ and _____

This leads to THREE propositions, which are tested in this study. Complete the table below:

1	If a person experiences a state of arousal for which they have no immediate explanation, they will label this state and describe their feelings in terms of the _____available to them. The same state of arousal could be labelled as 'joy' or 'anger' or 'jealousy' depending on the_____ the person is in.
2	If a person experiences a state of arousal for which they have an appropriate explanation, they will be _____ to label their feelings in terms of the alternative cognitions available.
3	In a situation which contains 'emotional cues', a person will react emotionally or experience emotions only if they are in a state of _____.

There are TWO INDEPENDENT VARIABLES in this study. The first one was the *STATE OF PHYSIOLOGICAL AROUSAL* and the second one was the *EXPLANATION* (or cognition) that an individual will give to this arousal.

All the subjects were given an injection that they were told was a vitamin called suproxin so that the researchers could look at its effect on visual skills. The explanation for their state of physiological arousal was manipulated by the information they were given at this time. There were four conditions. Read the descriptions below and label each one:

Description of condition	Label?
Subjects were given an adrenaline injection and not told of any effects of the drug.	
Subjects were given an adrenaline injection and warned of the 'side-effects' (hands shaking, heart pounding, dry mouth).	
Subjects were given an adrenaline injection and told to expect side-effects of numb feet and headache.	
Subjects were given an injection that would have no effect and were given no information about what to expect.	

What do Schachter and Singer propose will be the difference between the 'ignorant' and the 'informed' groups?

Explanations for their state of physiological arousal was further manipulated by assigning subjects to one of TWO conditions. Explain what happened in each condition.

ANGER CONDITION	EUPHORIA CONDITION

Emotional response was measured by OBSERVATION and SELF REPORT.

Give one *weakness* with the use of observation in this study.

What were the two 'critical' self-report questions?

Give one *weakness* with the use of self report in this study.

> The results graph looks very complicated! The data in the graph is a 'happiness minus anger' score. Answer the following questions about the results.

EUPHORIA SITUATIONS

Which groups show the greatest happiness?

Which groups show the least happiness?

> This SUPPORTS / DOES NOT SUPPORT Proposition 1.
>
> This SUPPORTS / DOES NOT SUPPORT Proposition 2.

The difference between the ignorant and the misinformed groups was not significant.

> This SUPPORTS / DOES NOT SUPPORT Proposition 3.

ANGER SITUATIONS (Note: results refer to observers' ratings due to concern that subjects would not give truthful responses about anger as taking part in the study earned them course credits.)

Which group showed the most anger?

> Which proposition does this support? Explain your answer.

- Was this study ETHICAL? Should it have been done?

Schachter and Singer's TWO-FACTOR THEORY of emotion proposes that emotion comes from a combination of:

AROUSAL AND COGNITION

1 | If a person experiences a state of arousal for which they have no immediate explanation, they will label this state and describe their feelings in terms of the COGNITIONS available to them. The same state of arousal could be labelled as 'joy' or 'anger' or 'jealousy' depending on the SITUATION the person is in.

2 | If a person experiences a state of arousal for which they have an appropriate explanation, they will be UNLIKELY to label their feelings in terms of the alternative cognitions available.

3 | In a situation which contains 'emotional cues', a person will react emotionally or experience emotions only if they are in a state of AROUSAL.

Description of condition	Label
Subjects were given an adrenaline injection and not told of any effects of the drug.	IGNORANT
Subjects were given an adrenaline injection and warned of the 'side-effects' (hands shaking, heart pounding, dry mouth).	INFORMED
Subjects were given an adrenaline injection and told to expect side-effects of numb feet and headache.	MISINFORMED
Subjects were given an injection that would have no effect and were given no information about what to expect.	PLACEBO

IDEAS FOR GROUP / INDIVIDUAL ACTIVITIES

● Was this study ETHICAL? Review your copy of the ethical guidelines for research for human participants and assess Schachter and Singer's research (remember, this study was conducted around the same time as Milgram's obedience experiments and before the introduction of ethical guidelines).

This is a straightforward activity which should not require much guidance. The key issue is deception and there are quite a few examples of this in this Core Study.

A similar activity could be conducted where you ask students to consider some of the **methodological problems** with this study. This might include the fact that participants were students offered extra course credits for participating and the effect that this might have had on their responses (particularly in respect of the angry stooge), the way in which emotion was measured, the 'missing' condition and so on.

● Imagine that you were a participant in this experiment. How might you feel about having taken part?

You could make this more interesting by dividing the students into the same groups as the original experiment (epi informed, epi ignorant etc. and the euphoria and anger situations) and ask group to consider their feelings separately and then feedback their ideas to the rest of the class.

● Schachter and Singer were trying to discover how much our emotional responses are physiological and how much they are cognitive (based on an interpretation of what is going on around us). Keep this in mind and try to design an ethical (or a more ethical one than Schachter and Singer's) investigation of this idea.

This is a harder activity and perhaps one to be avoided if your students have struggled with this Core Study. If you decide to try this, it would probably be best to discuss ways of investigating / manipulating positive emotions as this would be considered more ethical than the manipulation of negative emotions. This is clearly only a design exercise – although students may come up with some interesting ideas, they will be far too complex and time consuming for Unit 2542!

Dement and Kleitman

TEACHING NOTES

This Core Study was published in 1957, making it one of the oldest in the current specification. It is important to point this out to students as this study represents an important breakthrough in the history of sleep research. Also, much of what can be found in textbooks today was not known when Dement and Kleitman conducted this research.

This study does not attempt to research questions such as why we sleep or why we dream but focuses on **three questions** relating simply to **the relationship between eye movement and dreaming**.

It is not necessary for students to have very much background to this study (they will understand it with the minimum of introduction) but if you have time, there are some interesting topics to consider.

You could consider theories of why we sleep, or you could simply consider some of the case studies of sleep deprivation. You could take a slightly different approach and consider theories of dreaming and possibly make links between this Core Study and the Core Study by Freud, which has some material on dream interpretation. These topics are covered in most introductory textbooks (see Gross, Gross and McIlveen). Whichever approach you decide to take, make sure that students are aware that they do not have to learn all of this material. They will simply be examined on their knowledge of the Core Study.

There are several straightforward evaluation issues that can be considered in relation to this study. The major one to consider is the ecological validity of sleeping in a laboratory (see Group tasks) and you could also ask students to consider alternative explanations for some of the results.

PSYCHOLOGICAL INVESTIGATIONS

This Core Study may generate a number of ideas for data collecting exercises (see later in this book). Students generally find the topics of sleep and dreaming interesting ones and may be keen to study related areas.

For example: **questionnaire / self report** research may be conducted on sleep habits (number of hours' sleep, difficulty sleeping etc.) or dream recall (do people remember their dreams, do they believe dreams have meanings etc.?). Steer students away from asking overly personal questions such as the content of dreams as they may be embarrassed by these questions.

An **observation** may be conducted (with participants' consent) into how alert or tired people appear to be in class. For example, students could design a checklist of behaviours (yawning, closing eyes, putting head down on desk etc.) to observe with a psychology class. Perhaps you could use **self report** measures for this as well and then **correlate** the two.

A **comparison of two conditions** could be conducted where people are divided into two groups on the basis of the number of hours' sleep they had the previous night (six hours or less and more than six hours, for example) and they could then be tested in some way (memory, EWT, reaction time etc.). This type of task could also be conducted as a **correlation** where number of hours' sleep is correlated against a measure of some cognitive skill.

Dement, W. and Kleitman, N. (1957)

The relation of eye movements during sleep to dream activity: an objective method for the study of dreaming. *Journal of Experimental Psychology,* **53, 339–346**

This is a very early study of dreaming based on the observation that people have long periods of Rapid Eye Movement (REM) when they are asleep. It was suggested that these periods of REM might correlate with dreaming.

NOTE: this study does *not* attempt to answer questions about the reasons why we dream or to explain what our dreams mean.

This study had THREE research questions:

QUESTION 1

QUESTION 2

QUESTION 3

Who were the *participants* in this study?

Outline the *procedure* for this study and comment on the *ecological validity* of this.

Did all the participants show REM?

Describe THREE characteristics of REM sleep.

1

2

3

What does an EEG record? Outline *one problem* with using an EEG to investigate dreaming.

Research question 1: *Does dream recall correlate with periods of REM?*

Subjects were woken at various points during the night by a doorbell. They then had to speak into a tape recorder, stating whether or not they had been dreaming and if they had, describing the content of their dream.

Why did the researchers use a doorbell?

How *many times* in total were the subjects woken from REM sleep?

In what *percentage* of these awakenings did participants report dreams?

How *many times* in total were the subjects woken from N-REM sleep?

In what *percentage* of these awakenings did participants report dreams?

Evaluate the *criteria* used for recording when a dream had taken place.

Looking at the above results, do you think that they support research question 1 or not?

Research question 2: *Correlation between estimate of dream length and time in REM?*

Summarise the results of the study into estimation of dream length.

Time in REM	5 mins		15 mins	
estimate	correct	incorrect	correct	incorrect
total				

Does this support research question 2 or not?

Research question 3: *Is type of eye movement related to content of dream?*

Describe the FOUR patterns of REM that the researchers looked for and give an example of the type of dream that might have been occurring.

Does this support research question 3 or not?

THE THREE RESEARCH QUESTIONS

Q1	Does dream recall correlate with periods of REM?
Q2	Is there a correlation between the estimate of dream length and the time spent in REM?
Q3	Is the type of eye movement related to the content of the dream?

CHARACTERISTICS OF REM SLEEP

- Occur at regular intervals (average = every 90 min)

- Last between 3 and 50 mins

- Increase in length during the night

- Accompanied by particular EEG patterns (low voltage, fast).

IDEAS FOR GROUP / INDIVIDUAL ACTIVITIES

● Draw up a table comparing sleeping in your own bed with sleeping in a laboratory. To what extent do you think that sleeping in a laboratory has ecological validity?

Students should be able to think of lots of answers for this and the exercise could be done with the whole class, with the ideas written on the board. I would expect that the answer to the second question would be that sleeping in a laboratory would have low ecological validity but some students may argue otherwise.

● Has your alarm clock ever turned into a fire alarm in your dream?

A study conducted by Dement and Wolpert (1958) attempted to influence the content of participants' dreams by providing some external stimulation, for example by flashing lights or spraying them with cold water. They found that a number of the participants incorporated the stimulation into dreams such as spilling water on themselves.

Design a study which attempts to influence the content of participants' dreams. Give details of the procedure that you would follow and identify any practical or ethical problems that you might face.

This is an enjoyable exercise which will produce lots of silly ideas along the lines of the study by Dement and Wolpert! Let students generate lots of ideas like this and then spend some time considering the problems of this kind of research. These could range from practical and ethical problems associated with getting people to volunteer for this kind of research, or being angry when they were woken up, through to more methodological problems such as how to question them without leading them and so on.

● There have been several famous studies into sleep deprivation. Try to find out about the cases of Peter Tripp and Randy Gardner. What effects did they experience and how have these effects been explained?

This is obviously moving away from the AS specification but these cases (which are covered in all introductory textbooks) are fascinating and students generally enjoy finding out about them. If you have a spare hour, this would make an interesting activity and would allow you to talk about some of the more recent sleep and dreaming research which focuses on the cognitive aspects of dreaming.

Sperry

TEACHING NOTES

Before you look at the Core Study by Sperry, it will be necessary to give students some background material relating to **hemisphere specialisation**. They do not need a huge amount of detail but they do need some key points such as the following:

1   The brain is divided into two hemispheres, which have different functions.
2   The **left hemisphere** specialises in **verbal and symbolic functions** and the **right hemisphere** specialises in **visuo-spatial functions**.
3   The frequency and severity of **epileptic seizures** can be reduced if the fibres connecting the two hemispheres are cut. This operation is known as a **commissurotomy**. Patients who have had this operation are known as **split-brain patients**.
4   Sperry developed a **technique** which allowed the testing of each hemisphere separately. He was able to use this technique to study some of the patients that had had this operation and through his studies is able to provide us with some definitive answers about **hemispheric specialisation**.

This is quite straightforward and this should allow you to introduce the study in a relatively easy way for non-science students. You will need to spend some time making sure that they understand how information is transmitted to each hemisphere (right hand to left hemisphere etc.) and specifically that visual fields are not the same as eyes! Banyard explains this very clearly in *Introducing Psychological Research*:

> *Imagine looking straight ahead. Then the view to the right of your nose is the 'right visual field' and the view to the left of your nose is the 'left visual field'. The nerves of the visual system are arranged in such a way that the view of the left visual field goes to the right hemisphere of the brain and the view from the right visual field goes to the left hemisphere of the brain.*

Visual information can thus be **manipulated** by blindfolding one of the participant's eyes (this is where the confusion comes in: it is simpler to control visual fields in just one eye than two, but students often misunderstand this as covering up one eye and flashing the information to the other), getting them to fixate with the seeing eye on a point in the middle of a screen and then flashing information on either the right or the left side of this fixation point for less than 1/10 of a second. If it were flashed for longer, then there is every likelihood that the person's eyes would move and the information would be transmitted to both visual fields and hence to both hemispheres. Manipulation of **tactile information** is simpler: so long as the person's hands are out of sight, it is simply a matter of allowing only one hand to touch the item.

This is initially all very complex for students, but once they grasp the basic concepts the findings of the study are relatively straightforward. If you draw a very simple diagram of two hemispheres on the board with arrows connecting the eyes and hands, it should be easy for students to work out where each piece of information goes. Getting them to think in terms of 'two brains' may make this easier.

Sperry, R.W. (1968)

Hemisphere deconnection and unity in consciousness. *American Psychologist,* **23, 723–733**

Explain what is meant by a *'split-brain'*.

For what *reason* did people have this operation?

NOTE: The 11 subjects who took part in this study had undergone this operation for the reasons you have outlined above – NOT for the sake of the experiment!

Why do you think these people are of so much interest to psychologists?

Explain the *techniques* used by Sperry to present information to only one side of the brain.

Read the *results section* of this article and then answer the following questions:

1   If a subject was presented with an image in one half of their visual field and then the same image was *re-shown to the other half of the visual field*, did they recognise this as something they had seen before? Explain your answer.

2   Give one piece of evidence that illustrates the language limitations of the *right hemisphere* of the brain.

3   Give one piece of evidence that illustrates that this same hemisphere is not completely word blind.

4 Two symbols are presented simultaneously, one to each side of the brain.

£ to right visual field

$ to left visual field

The subjects' hands are screened from sight.

If asked to draw with left hand what they have just seen, which symbol will they draw?

If asked what they have just drawn, what will they reply?

Explain why this happens.

5 Subjects have their hands screened from sight and an object placed in their right hand and then removed. They are asked to search for the object with the same hand. Can they find it? Why?

6 If an object is put in the left hand (screened) what is the person not able to do?

What did Sperry find in tasks requiring *parallel responses*?

Explain how the patients *coped* with this lack of communication between the hemispheres in everyday life.

Would it be appropriate to make *generalisations* about *normal brain* functioning from these studies? Explain your answer.

IDEAS FOR GROUP / INDIVIDUAL ACTIVITIES

● It could be argued that some of the effects demonstrated by Sperry are 'experimental artefacts': that is, they occur only in these very controlled conditions. What real life problems might be experienced by someone with a 'split-brain' and how might they overcome these problems?

This is an interesting issue to consider. In real life, visual information would go to both visual fields and holding something in one hand without being able to see what you are doing would be rare! Sperry reports that the participants often reverted to speaking out loud to themselves in order to transfer information from one hemisphere to the other. This would suggest that there are only a few occasions when they would experience real problems. Students have suggested things like eye tests, driving and other technical activities as ones where people might have problems. It would be interesting to see what other suggestions your students can come up with. Someone once told me that a student of theirs had asked if people with split-brains have two dreams at the same time and this also raises the question of whether both hemispheres would fall asleep at the same time.

● What problems might there be in generalising from the results of this study? In other words, should we accept the results of this study as telling us anything about 'normal' brain functioning?

This is a fairly quick issue to consider. Obviously we should be cautious about generalising from such a small group of people, but you could also suggest that there might be other differences between the brain functioning of people who have suffered such extreme seizures and then have had this operation and other people. Any study which generalises from atypical cases to typical ones should be considered carefully.

● Psychologists are interested in people like the subjects of this Core Study as it provides them with the opportunity to study aspects of behaviour which would otherwise be *impossible* (for practical or ethical reasons). What other naturally occurring cases might be of interest of psychologists and why?

Again, this is a quick activity and could be done in five minutes with the whole class. Some suggestions to get you started include cases where people have had their sight restored after being blind since birth and any issues relating to the severe deprivation of children (Genie would be an excellent example here).

Raine, Buchsbaum and LaCasse

TEACHING NOTES

You might find that you spend a great deal of time on this study and give students a great deal of knowledge about brain structures and functions that they may find complex and confusing. It is possible to consider all of the important issues raised by this study without having to deal with an enormous amount of neurophysiology.

Basically, this is a study which uses a relatively new technique (**PET scans**) to try to identify whether people who are pleading Not Guilty by Reason of Insanity to a charge of murder have **different patterns of brain functioning** from those of non-murderers. This locates the study firmly within the 'nature' end of the **nature-nurture debate** and this may be a good place to start. You could ask students to consider **reasons** why someone might commit a crime such as murder and then identify the different perspectives and introduce this study as looking for a biological cause. If you are planning to teach A2 Psychology and Crime, this debate will appear again next year.

The task that the participants were asked to do was a simple **target recognition task** and the results showed significant differences in certain areas of the brain. This suggests that the brains of the murderers somehow work differently from the non-murderers' but does not offer proof that this is related to the act of murder.

Very simply, the results showed:

1   **Reduced glucose metabolism in prefrontal cortex, posterior cortex and corpus callosum.**
2   **Abnormal asymmetries of activity (left lower than right) in the amygdala, thalamus and hippocampus.**

Raine explains that damage to the prefrontal cortex can result in **impulsivity, immaturity, altered emotionality, loss of self-control and the inability to modify behaviour.** All of these may increase the likelihood of aggressive acts. The amygdala is associated with **aggressive behaviour** and also the **recognition of emotional stimuli such as a fearful expression on someone's face.** Damage to the amygdala is associated with **fearlessness.** The part of the limbic system made up of the amygdala, hippocampus and prefrontal cortex governs the **expression of emotion.** Together with the thalamus, these areas are important in learning, memory and attention, and the suggestion is made that abnormal functioning may lead to problems such as not being able to form conditioned emotional responses and the failure to learn from experiences.

Note that this does not mean that Raine, Buchsbaum and LaCasse have demonstrated a **causal link** between this patterning of functioning and murder, and there are many other factors that might be implicated.

The focus for discussion should be:

1   **The problems associated with PET scans (what they do or do not tell us).**
2   **The ethical implications of this type of research (see Application of Psychology to everyday life for a very clear discussion of the implications).**

Raine, A., Buchsbaum, M. and LaCasse, L. (1997)

Brain abnormalities in murderers indicated by positron emission tomography. *Biological Psychiatry*, 42 (6), 495–508

PET stands for POSITRON EMISSION TOMOGRAPHY. PET scans allow researchers to examine the relationship between activity in the brain and mental processes. PET works by measuring the level of metabolic activity occurring within the brain. Someone having a PET scan is first injected with a small amount of harmless radioactive material 'bonded' to a substance such as glucose. Since the brain's primary form of energy is glucose, the areas which are most active absorb more of it. The glucose is broken down by the brain but the radioactive material is not, and as it decays it emits positively charged particles called positrons which are detected by the scan. This information is then fed to a computer which produces different coloured images of the level of activity occurring throughout the brain, different colours indicating different levels of activity.

PET scans can be used to:

- Provide images of what is going on in the brain DURING various BEHAVIOURS (an advantage over other scanning techniques such as CAT and MRI scans).
- Identify those areas of the brain that are active when we are THINKING. For example, different brain activity has been found in response to the instructions 'move your right hand' and 'think about moving your right hand'.
- Locate tumours and growths (to provide vital information about the likelihood of essential brain structures being damaged by surgery).
- Reveal possible differences between the brains of people with and without psychological disorders (some differences have been found between the brains of schizophrenics and non-schizophrenics – supporting the notion that this disorder has a physical cause).
- Explore differences between the sexes. Gur *et al.*, 1995 showed that men have a more active metabolism than women in the primitive brain centres that control sex and violence.

In this study PET scans are used to investigate the notion that there were differences in *brain activity* between 41 murderers (39 male and two female, mean age = 34.3) pleading Not Guilty by Reason of Insanity (NGRI) and 41 controls (screened for mental and physical health).

The participants had to work at a continuous performance task based around target recognition for 32 minutes and were then given the PET scan. *Evaluate* the selection of task, remembering what the aim of this study was!

The researchers found that there was *less activity in the corpus callosum* of the NGRI group compared to the controls. What characteristics are associated with low levels of activity in this part of the brain?

The researchers found that there was an *imbalance of activity in the amygdala* (less activity in the left side and more in the right side of the NGRI group). What characteristics are associated with this kind of imbalance?

What *other differences* did the researchers find in the brain activity of the NGRI group compared to the controls?

There are a number of problems associated with the data produced by PET scans. Outline THREE of these problems.

<blockquote>
The researchers offer two tentative conclusions:
1 They suggest that the research supports previous findings relating to the role of the amygdala in violent behaviour (imbalance in activity = unusual emotional responses and lack of fear).
2 They suggest that the difference in corpus callosum activity may have similarities with research conducted on people with 'split-brains' (see Sperry) which shows them to have inappropriate emotional expression and the inability to grasp the long-term implications of a situation.
</blockquote>

However, the researchers are *very cautious indeed* about the implications of their findings. There are FOUR key points here:

1

2

3

4

<blockquote>
It should also be noted that imaging techniques are still being developed and any data produced in this way should be treated with caution. The relevance of the task has already been noted. Finally, the issue of violent and non-violent murder is raised: is murder always a violent act? This has *not* been controlled for.
</blockquote>

PROBLEMS WITH PET SCANS

- Generation of images is very complex – scope for errors / wishful thinking

- Hotspots of activity could be excitatory nerves (the 'on' switch) or inhibitory nerves (the 'off' switch) – activity looks the same to the scan

- As the brain becomes practised at a task, the amount of activity declines: therefore 'hotspots' may not be something important but simply something new

- Imaging techniques are still in the developmental stage and we should treat the data with caution.

THE FINDINGS

- DO NOT show that violence is caused by biology

- DO NOT show that that NGRIs are not responsible for their actions

- DO NOT tell us anything about the cause of the brain differences

- CANNOT be generalised to other offenders or to other types of crimes.

IDEAS FOR GROUP / INDIVIDUAL ACTIVITIES

● Should we apply the results of this Core Study to the identification of potential murderers or to looking for ways to treat murderers? Give reasons for your answer.

This is basically asking students to consider the ethical implications of this Core Study. If we used this to identify people with pattern of brain functioning but who had never committed an aggressive act, what could we do with this information? It is not difficult to imagine a world where this kind of information could have devastating consequences. This could easily be linked to the discussion of labelling in relation to the Core Study by Rosenhan.

● Are people born criminals? What do you think? Make a list of all the factors that you can think of that might lead somebody to do something criminal.

This is a useful exercise if you are planning to teach Psychology and Crime next year or if you feel that the nature–nurture debate needs revision! Your students should be able to generate a large number of ideas for this which will span the nature–nurture debate. If you have time to extend this activity, you could ask students to consider which, if any, of these factors should be taken into consideration by courts when deciding on punishments. You may be surprised by their attitudes!

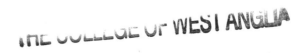

The social approach
Milgram

TEACHING NOTES

This is often selected as the first study to teach and there are arguments for and against this. It obviously is a fascinating study to begin with and students will find discussing the study fairly easy. If you want to introduce **ethics** early on in the course then you can do so in relation to this study. However, this study is not typical of psychological research and may give students a less than accurate impression of the rest of the course. You may also find that you have a more useful discussion of the many issues raised by the study later in the course. It is also difficult to introduce some elements of **research methodology** using this study. Although you can discuss the ecological validity of laboratory conditions and the study involves some good examples of experimental control (same prompts, same responses from learner at same shock levels etc.), it is difficult to identify exactly what the independent variable is here and there is no control group. In fact, it has been suggested that this Core Study may be better understood as a controlled observation. You may find that the choice of a **very simple experimental design** such as Loftus and Palmer is an easier introduction for your students.

This Core Study is the first of Milgram's many obedience studies. It is important that you are aware of this as Milgram conducted many variations on this basic method and the results vary slightly from study to study. You need to concentrate on the procedure and the results of this study so that students in the examination do not describe slight variations. Having said this, it is worth considering the **variations,** especially when you are discussing the factors that led to obedience in this study. For example, when Milgram repeated the study in a less prestigious environment, obedience dropped, which supports the notion that the original environment (Yale University) did contribute to the high levels of obedience. These variations are described in several general textbooks (see *Gross Psychology: The Science of Mind and Behaviour 4th edition*, 2001, pages 394–95 for a good account of these).

You should also consider the **social context** of the study with your students. This could include the Nazi war trials as well as the nature of 1960s society and the changes that may have taken place since then. You could ask students to consider if the same results would be found again if you were to replicate the study. The halovine video listed in **Resources**, page 11, outlines this at the start of the video.

Milgram, S. (1963)

Behavioural study of obedience. *Journal of Abnormal and Social Psychology, 67, 371–378*

The article reports on the *original* study conducted by Milgram. He conducted several variations on this procedure which we will look at briefly later. His work is one of the most *controversial* pieces of research in Psychology.

What is meant by the term 'obedience'?

Give some examples of *real life obedience to authority*.

Why did Milgram conduct this research?

Who were the *subjects* for this study and how did Milgram obtain them?

What are the *disadvantages* of this method of selecting subjects?

Briefly outline the procedure for this study.

Hints:

'drawing lots'

information about shocks

word pairs

prods

Complete the following results table:

Voltage	270	285	300	315	330	345	360	375	390	405	420	435	450
No of Ps obeying													

Convert the number of people continuing to 450 volts into a percentage.

What happened at 300 volts that may have led some subjects to stop?

Milgram states that the study created tension in the subjects. What evidence is there for this statement?

Milgram 'debriefed' his subjects. What did the debriefing consist of?

Milgram suggests nine features of the study that may have contributed to the high levels of obedience. Make a note of each one and see if you can think of any more.

1

2

3

4

5

6

7

8

9

any more?

WHY DID PEOPLE OBEY?

- The study was conducted at a prestigious university (Yale)

- The experimenter was perceived as an authority figure

- The subjects had been paid and may have felt obligated

- They were told that the shocks were not harmful

- The learners consented and were answering up until the twentieth shock.

What other reasons can you think of?

IDEAS FOR GROUP / INDIVIDUAL ACTIVITIES

● Read the handout on *Ethical guidelines for psychological research.* Imagine that these guidelines had been in place when Milgram conducted his research. Which guidelines did he break?

The guidelines were not in place when Milgram conducted his research. Ethical guidelines were introduced soon afterwards. Clearly there are many aspects of Milgram's research which break these guidelines. Probably the most important ones are:

Deception: there are several examples of deception: that the learner was a confederate, that the draw had been rigged, that no shocks were actually being given, that the 'subject' of the research was actually the teacher and so on.

Protection of participants: Milgram failed to protect his participants from psychological harm. Apart from the obvious stress experienced by the participants at the time of the research, there are issues regarding the long-term effects of having taken part in this study.

You could also use this exercise to introduce the notion of **debriefing** if you have not considered this yet. Milgram did debrief his participants very thoroughly and followed this up months later to ensure that no lasting harm had been done. He reports that participants were glad to have taken part in the study. This could lead you to consider whether debriefing makes up for unethical aspects of research or not. You could also consider whether participants will say that they were glad to have taken part as this will reduce the cognitive dissonance experienced by obeying.

Depending on time, you could also ask students to consider whether the research should have been conducted at all. Some of the arguments **for** the research might be: Milgram asked a number of people to anticipate the results of this study and most people estimated between 0.1% and 1% of people would obey. This makes the results even more unexpected and therefore **useful** to psychologists. The study tells us something very important about human nature and challenges our strongly held assumptions about it. Milgram puts forward an eloquent defence on his research in his book *Obedience to Authority*. In this book he argues that critics of his work write as if the production of stress in our subjects was an intended effect of the experimental manipulation. He responds:

> There are many laboratory procedures specifically designed to create stress (Lazurus 1964), but the obedience paradigm was not one of them. The extreme tension induced in some subjects was unexpected. Before conducting the experiment, the procedures were discussed with many colleagues and none anticipated the reactions that subsequently took place. Foreknowledge of results can never be the invariable accompaniment of an experimental probe. Understanding grows because we examine situations in which the end is unknown. An investigator unwilling to accept this degree of risk must give up the idea of scientific risk. (page 212)

You could counter this claim with arguments about the **rights of participants** and with the argument that once it was clear that participants were locked into the 'agentic state', Milgram could have terminated the research rather than subjecting them to any more stress. You could also consider the numerous replications of this research that have been conducted (both by Milgram and others) and whether these can be justified.

This would make an excellent **debate** between students who are developing their skills of evaluation (so may be less appropriate if this is the first Core Study you have taught them).

Divide the class into two groups – one arguing that the research can be justified and one arguing that it cannot. If you are feeling mean you could deliberately put people in a group where they have to argue against the points they have expressed so far – it will do them good to consider the opposite point of view.

- Comment on the *ecological validity* of this research – can the results be generalised to 'real life'?

This will no doubt be a much shorter exercise than the one above and possibly less contentious. It would also be suitable for students studying this Core Study at the start of their course.

You could consider the following points:

- The relationship between the teacher and the experimenter

- The fact that the participants volunteered

- The payment

- The environment in which the research took place

- Any possible consequences for disobedience.

You may find that whilst you can argue very convincingly that this study is conducted in an environment very different from 'real life', there are many overlaps. In any work situation, for example, the factors above are magnified. You may obey your boss because you are scared you will lose your job, with major financial consequences, and so on. I think it is likely that some students might consider that this study has high ecological validity (the participants believed it was real), others may consider the ecological validity to be low. As long as they can justify their position, this is fine. Both arguments can be backed up with examples and evidence from the study.

- Look up the studies by Hofling (1966) and by Sheridan and King (1972). What did they find? What conclusions can be drawn from these studies?

These studies should be familiar to you and can be found in most introductory textbooks. The Hofling study looked at obedience in a real life setting (nurses in a hospital) and the Sheridan and King study asked participants to give electric shocks to a puppy. Both studies found very high levels of obedience. You could set this as a research exercise: one group to research each study and present it to the rest of the class. Ask students to consider the following questions in relation to each of these studies:

Are the results more or less frightening than the Milgram study?
Are these studies more or less unethical than the Milgram study?

- Imagine that you were a participant in the Milgram study.

This could be done as a quick task at the end of discussing the study or could be extended into a full activity. If you want to spend some time on this you could give the students a series of questions to consider, such as the following:

How do you think you would feel arriving at Yale University?
How do you think you would feel when drawing lots?
How do you think you would feel when watching the learner being 'strapped in' and hearing what they had to do?
How do you think you would feel when you were given the sample shock?
How do you think you would feel when you started reading the word pairs?
How do you think you would feel when you had to give the first electric shock?
How do you think you would feel when the learner started screaming?
How do you think you would feel when the learner stopped responding?
How do you think you would feel when the experimenter refused to let you stop and refused to check on the learner?
How do you think you would feel when you were told that 'the experiment must be discontinued'?
How do you think you would feel when you found out that you had been deceived?

There are lots of questions here, but working through them will give students some idea of the range of emotions that the participants must have felt, as well as illustrating how long the experiment went on for.

Haney, Banks and Zimbardo

TEACHING NOTES

This is a fascinating study which has many applications. The funding for the study came from the US Navy and the study was published in the *Naval Research Review*. This suggests that there was a focus on the conditions and effects of prisoner of war camps rather than ordinary prisons. The original article is well worth reading, although the style is very academic and it is not always easy to follow. The authors locate the study firmly within the 'individual–situational' debate, as this quote demonstrates:

> there is the contention that violence and brutality exist within prison because guards are
> sadistic, uneducated and insensitive people. It is the 'guard mentality', a unique syndrome of
> negative traits which they bring into the situation, that engenders the inhumane treatment
> of prisoners. On the other hand there is the argument that prison violence and brutality are
> the logical and predictable results of the involuntary confinement of a collective of
> individuals whose life histories are, by definition, characterised by disregard for law, order
> and social convention and a concurrent propensity for impulsivity and aggression ...

With some explanation, this quote would serve as an excellent introduction to the study. It clearly outlines a **dispositional (individual)** explanation for the behaviours found within prisons. As the authors explain, these explanations are used by those who support the current prison system (blaming the 'evil' prisoners) and those who condemn the current system (blaming the 'evil' guards). This analysis directs attention away from the **environment or situation** in which this all takes place. This allows the system to continue unchecked.

You could ask students to think of ways in which these ideas could be tested, although this is a difficult task. Zimbardo points out that testing these ideas by **observation** would not be possible and that it is therefore necessary to **construct a prison environment** populated by 'individuals who are undifferentiated in all essential dimensions from the rest of society'. You could ask students to think of reasons why observation would not be appropriate and why you would need to populate a mock prison with people who are 'undifferentiated' from the rest of society.

Zimbardo describes his prison as less of a 'literal' simulation of a prison and more of a 'functional' representation of one. He explains that for ethical, moral and pragmatic reasons they did not allow the threat of severe physical punishment, for example, but that they aimed to create the same feelings of power and powerlessness, of control and oppression, of satisfaction and frustration, of arbitrary rule and resistance to authority, of status and anonymity, of *machismo* and emasculation.

The **hypothesis** was a general one: **that assignment to the group 'prisoner' or 'guard' would result in significant differences in behaviour.**

There are numerous **websites** devoted to this study but probably the best one is Zimbardo's own site (www.zimbardo.com) which contains a link to actual video footage of the study together with a detailed examination of all aspects of the study. The *Stanford News* (a university newspaper) published an article on this study titled 'The Stanford prison experiment: still powerful after all these years' (1997). In it there are quotes from Christina Maslach (a respected psychologist, Zimbardo's wife and his girlfriend at the time of the study) outlining her horror at the rapid development of the study. Her response to what she saw five days after the start of the study was the impetus for the halting of the study soon afterwards. This article is well worth reading and can be found online at: www2.stanford.edu/dept/news/relaged/970108prisonexp.html.

Haney, C., Banks, W.C. and Zimbardo, P.G. (1973)

A study of prisoners and guards in a simulated prison. *Naval Research Review,* 30, 4–17.

This is often referred to as the 'Zimbardo' experiment as Philip Zimbardo was the lead researcher on this project.

What was the AIM of this research?

Naval Research Review is not a psychological journal! Explain why this research was published here.

Explain how the *participants* for this study were selected.

Why do you think the participants had to be *randomly assigned* their roles as either prisoners or guards?

Mock Prison: this was created in the basement of the Psychology Department Building at Stanford University. It was made up of three cells (each 6ft by 9ft) with three prisoners to a cell, and a solitary confinement cell (a cupboard 2ft by 2ft by 7ft). There were guards' rooms etc. in an adjacent building. There was also a small enclosed room used as a prison yard which had an observation window concealing video equipment and observers.

What information were the participants given prior to the start of the study?

Outline the 'arrest' procedure used in this study. What effect do you think this would have had on the participants who were to play the prisoners?

Describe the uniforms worn by both prisoners and guards and the roles they had to play:

Guard's uniform	Role / rules
Prisoner's uniform	**Role / rules**

Outline the effect of the simulated prison on the *prisoners*:

Outline the effect of the simulated prison on the *guards*:

What is the evidence that these were 'real' effects rather than role-playing?

Explain what Zimbardo means by the term *'pathological prisoner syndrome'*. What processes contributed to this?

Guard's uniform

Khaki shirt and trousers

Whistle

Police night stick (wooden baton)

Mirror sunglasses

Role / rules

'To maintain the reasonable degree of order within the prison necessary for its effective functioning'

Worked 8 hour shifts and went home after each shift

Prisoner's uniform

Loose-fitting smock with number on front and back

No underwear

Light chain and lock around ankle

Rubber sandals

Nylon stocking cap

Role / rules

Referred to only by number

Allowed 3 supervised toilet visits per day

2 hours 'privileges'

2 visits per week

Work assignments

'Count' at start of each guard shift

IDEAS FOR GROUP / INDIVIDUAL ACTIVITIES

- **Comment on the ethics of the study. Should it have been conducted? Should it have been stopped?**

You could do this as a very similar exercise to the one proposed for the Core Study by Milgram. Ensure that students have a copy of the **Ethical guidelines** (page 31) and ask them to consider which guidelines, if any, were broken. This could be structured as a debate with one group arguing that the study should have been conducted and one arguing that the study should not have been conducted. If you used the debate idea for the previous Core Study (Milgram) you could put people in the opposite groups this time.

Should it have been stopped? This is a complex issue. Was Zimbardo right to call a halt to this study? He feels that the decision to call a halt to the experiment after six days was justified, although others might argue that it should have been stopped sooner, or even that it should have been allowed to continue for longer. As with many of these questions, there are no right answers, but this Core Study provides a good vehicle for the process of formulating an opinion and backing it up.

- **How realistic was the study? Suggest similarities and differences between this and a real prison.**

This exercise is also very similar to the one suggested for the previous study on ecological validity. Whenever I have done this with students I have been surprised at the range of different opinions. Some argue persuasively that this study is very realistic because of the effects that it had on the participants, and others argue equally persuasively that the participants knew that this was a mock prison and therefore it has very low ecological validity. Both positions are valid ones and it is an interesting exercise to discover their opinions.

If you have access to the BBC's 2002 television series, 'The Experiment', this would make a good classroom exercise. Show students a clip of the Zimbardo study if you have one (or use the website) and then an extract from 'The Experiment'. Ask them to consider all the ways in which the two prisons differed. They will probably be able to do this quite easily although you could point them in the direction of the actual environment, the uniforms for both prisoners and guards and the fact that the participants in 'The Experiment' knew that they were on television.

- **De-individuation is the 'loss of personal identity' which was seen in this study. In what other situations do people become de-individuated?**

This is probably best as a short task at the end of a lesson rather than a large-scale activity. Some ideas include any jobs where people wear uniforms, any crowd situation (football crowds, concerts, demonstrations etc.), and you could also make links here with the Core Study by Rosenhan which touches on notions of institutionalisation.

- **An important debate in psychology is between *individual* and *social* explanations for behaviour. What does this study have to add to this debate?**

Note that this activity could also be used for the Core Study by Milgram.

This is the key issue, according to the Introduction by Haney, Banks and Zimbardo. This study would suggest that all the behaviours shown by the participants were caused by situational factors. The individual natures of the participants were 'lost' in the roles that they were given to play. This is a fairly straightforward issue for students to grasp although if you read more detail about the study or have access to any video material, there is some suggestion that one of the guards (nicknamed John Wayne) may have taken on the role of guard far more than any of the others and that his behaviour had a profound effect on the whole simulation. This might tip the argument back slightly towards the importance of individual factors.

What applications does this study have? What does this study suggest about the nature of prisons? What changes could be made to ensure that the undesirable effects seen in the study do not happen in real prisons?

This exercise is probably only worth doing if you have spare time or are intending to revisit this study in A2 Psychology and Crime. There are obvious suggestions about 'the pathology of power' and the effects that this had on the guards and 'de-individuation' and the related stressful effects that were experienced by prisoners.

Piliavin, Rodin and Piliavin

TEACHING NOTES

The social context of this research was the now infamous case of Kitty Genovese who was murdered in March 1964. The case was particularly shocking as the police investigations revealed that at least 38 people had watched the murder from the safety of their own homes and only one witness called the police after Kitty had been killed.

This case was the impetus for research into helping behaviour and the initial research (most of it laboratory based) generated the concept of bystander apathy (now more commonly referred to as bystander intervention) and the concept of diffusion of responsibility. Any general textbook will give you an introduction to these theories if you want to cover this with your students. A brief account will suffice and you could introduce this Core Study by explaining the nature of a field experiment and its strengths and weaknesses. This is the only field experiment on the AS specification and it is worth spending some time on. This will also give you a good introduction to the study as Piliavin, Rodin and Piliavin's results are quite different from most of the laboratory studies and you need to consider explanations for this.

The study also uses participant observation. There are two important points to make. Firstly it demonstrates that researchers may use more than one methodology in their research. In this case, both experimental and observational methods are being used. Secondly it demonstrates that observation is not simply a research method but is also a technique for collecting data. Observation is also used in this way in the Core Studies by Schachter and Singer and by Bandura, Ross and Ross.

Once you have introduced these ideas, the Core Study is quite straightforward. The key variables of **black / white** and **drunk / cane** are easy for students to understand and the results are presented simply. The use of models is a little more complex. However, the interesting point about this aspect of the study is that the models did not have to intervene, as members of the public helped in the majority of the trials. This is another example of the results being very different from laboratory studies in this area. Diffusion of responsibility did not seem to happen in this study and this is a good discussion exercise.

This is also a good study to ask students to imagine **conducting** (rather than imagining that they are participants, as is more common). In this study there are uneven numbers of each of the drunk / cane conditions because students acting as the victims were not prepared to act in the ways required – they found the 'drunk' condition more difficult to do. Discussing this can make the research seem very real to students as well as highlighting the practical problems associated with field research.

Piliavin, I.M., Rodin, J.A. and Piliavin, J. (1969)

Good Samaritanism: an underground phenomenon? *Journal of Personality and Social Psychology,* 13, 289–299

Previous research into bystander apathy (now referred to as bystander intervention) identified several key concepts:

Pluralistic ignorance　　*Diffusion of responsibility*　　*Cost of helping*

Most of the early studies were laboratory experiments. What are the major *disadvantages* in studying social behaviour in this way?

Piliavin, Rodin and Piliavin's study is a FIELD experiment. What *advantages* do you think that this has over a laboratory based experiment?

Overview of study: a male 'victim' collapses on the subway during a non-stop 7.5 minute journey, between the hours of 11am and 3pm on weekdays. Sometimes the victim is a white man and sometimes a black man. Sometimes he is sober but unsteady on his feet and walking with a cane. Sometimes he is drunk and carrying a bottle in a brown paper bag. Two female observers record what happens.

Identify the variables in this experiment:

Independent variables	Dependent variables

RESULTS

Display the results of this study in an appropriate graph. Make sure you add all the necessary labels!

How did the following variables affect helping?

Appearance of victim (drunk / cane)	
Race of victim	
Number of people on the train	

Did men or women offer the most help? How could you explain these results?

Why were there different numbers of trials for the drunk / cane conditions?

Why is there *no data* for the effect of the model?

What difference might it have made if:

the victim had been female (and sober)?

the victim had been female and drunk?

the victim had been a child or a very elderly person?

the victim had been with someone?

the study had been conducted on the street rather than on a non-stop train?

CONCLUSIONS

The diffusion of responsibility hypothesis predicts that as the number of bystanders increases, then the likelihood that any individual will help decreases. Do the results from this study support this hypothesis?

How do Piliavin, Rodin and Piliavin explain their results?

IDEAS FOR GROUP / INDIVIDUAL ACTIVITIES

● Review your copy of the *Ethical guidelines for psychological research.* Are there any ethical problems with this study? Consider whether this kind of psychological research is acceptable or not.

You may not want to do yet another exercise on ethics after looking at the Core Studies by Milgram and Haney, Banks and Zimbardo, but it may be useful to consider the different ethical issues raised by conducting field research rather than laboratory based research. The lack of consent and the possible distress caused to participants are the main areas to look at.

● Design a study of helping behaviour using a *different* research method (not a field experiment). Comment on the strengths and weaknesses of your design.

This would be a good research methods exercise. You could just let students design any type of study or you could divide them into groups and ask one group to design an observation, one group a questionnaire and another group a laboratory experiment. They could present their ideas to the rest of the class and identify the strengths and weaknesses associated with the type of design they have used.

Tajfel

TEACHING NOTES

You may want to introduce the notion of prejudice before you start this study. Explanations of prejudice tended to focus on personality factors (authoritarianism, dogmatism etc.) in the 1950s and 1960s and moved gradually to social factors (conformity, competition etc.) in the 1970s and 1980s. More recent theories focus on more socio-cognitive explanations such as **social identity theory**. Tajfel's research focuses on the influence of group membership and in particular the effect of **minimal groups**. Rather than looking at pre-existing groups, such as racial or social groups, Tajfel proposes that the mere perception of the existence of another group can produce discrimination through the development of **ingroup** and **outgroup** attitudes.

To introduce this study, you could ask students to write down all the groups that they belong to. They may need some help with this to start but once you have given them some examples they will probably be able to think of lots. You could extend this activity: for example, by asking them to rate how strongly they identify with each of these groups (perhaps on a scale of 1–10). Divide them into two groups for a quiz or a debate and ask them to consider how they feel about the group they are in, and how they feel about the other group. You may find that group identities develop fairly rapidly under such conditions.

This would be a very easy study to **replicate** with your class, perhaps using sweets rather than points to increase enthusiasm! There are lots of arbitrary ways you could divide a class into two groups; the ones from the Core Study were the use of an estimation task and preference for pictures (you can get colour postcards of a Klee and a Kandinsky from a museum and photocopy them onto acetate). Or you could use a more stable method such as girls against boys or preference for music, football teams or soap operas, to see if discrimination increases with group stability.

Note, though, that Tajfel deliberately chose an **arbitrary variable** to decide on the two groups – using preference for football teams might seem a more 'real' way of studying prejudice but it brings in a number of other variables which are difficult to control in laboratory conditions. Tajfel's choice of such an arbitrary variable was deliberate and shows us that discrimination can occur simply because people are aware of the existence of other groups. Social identity theory offers us an explanation for this effect. By increasing the desirability of the ingroup (or by reducing the desirability of the outgroup) we can enhance our own social identity / self image. The implication of such studies and their explanations is unfortunately that prejudice and discrimination are almost impossible to eradicate. Other research by Tajfel simply increases this conclusion, as he found that telling people they had simply been assigned to groups randomly had no effect and they still showed a strong ingroup preference.

The study has obvious applications to the issue of **ethnocentrism**. This kind of research may help to explain where ethnocentric attitudes and behaviour originate. However, such research may itself be ethnocentric. One interesting finding is that such preferences may not be shown in all cultures. Gross discusses research by Wetherall (1982) in which she discovered that Polynesian children in New Zealand were much more generous to outgroups reflecting their cultural norms which emphasise co-operation.

PSYCHOLOGICAL INVESTIGATIONS

There are many ways in which the issues of prejudice and discrimination could be investigated further. **Questionnaire research** could be conducted where one group of participants is given a passage to read about a person (for example, a fictional account of a crime) and a second group is given a passage to read which is identical in all but one detail. This could be the sex of the person, or the race, but you might like to research some more unusual ones such as names (which might infer class or race) or the areas in which people live, which could give your research some local applications. Participants could be asked to rate the likelihood of guilt or of re-offending, or could be asked to choose appropriate punishments / treatments from a list. I have conducted research like this in several parts of the country and have always found strong prejudices on the basis of address. This raises some very interesting issues to do with labelling and self-fulfilling prophecy which could be linked to the Core Study by Rosenhan. Note that this kind of research could also be appropriate for Activity C.

Tajfel, H. (1970)

Experiments in intergroup discrimination. *Scientific American,* **223,** 96–102

What *groups* do you belong to?

Group membership is thought by Tajfel and others to be a fundamental factor in the creation of prejudice and discrimination. Tajfel uses the terms ingroup and outgroup ('us' and 'them') in his discussions of discriminatory behaviour. In these studies he aims to show that discrimination can result from minimal groups as well as from well established groups.

Explain what Tajfel meant by a 'minimal group'.

EXPERIMENT 1

Who were the participants in this experiment?

How did the boys *think* that they had been assigned to groups and how were they *really* assigned?

The boys were then asked individually to give rewards of real money to the other boys in the experiment. They were given booklets with grids such as the one below:

Choice number	1	2	3	4	5
Boy 1	9	11	12	14	16
Boy 2	5	9	11	15	19

They were not given the names of the boys that they were allocating money to but they did know which *group* each boy was in. Which 'choice number' from the above grid do you think the boys would select in each of the following situations?

Condition	Description	Choice number?
Ingroup choice	Boy 1 and Boy 2 in the same group as you	
Outgroup choice	Boy 1 and Boy 2 in the other group	
Intergroup choice	Boy 1 in your group Boy 2 in the other group	

Tajfel was particularly interested in the results from the *intergroup choices*. Outline what he found.

EXPERIMENT 2

Who were the subjects and how did they *think* they were assigned to groups?

Again, the boys had to complete reward booklets but this time there were *THREE variables* that might have an effect on the boys' choices. Describe the three variables:

Variable	Description
Maximum joint profit	
Largest possible reward to ingroup	
Maximum difference	

In this study, all the grids referred to one boy in your group and one boy in the other group.

Choice number	1	2	3	4	5
Boy 1 (ingroup)	9	11	12	14	16
Boy 2 (outgroup)	5	9	11	15	19

From the grid above, identify the choice number that would give

1 Maximum joint profit?
2 Maximum difference?

Briefly outline the results of experiment 2.

What conclusions can be drawn from this study about the necessary conditions for discrimination?

SAMPLE

This study was conducted on 14- and 15-year-old boys. What effect do you think this might have had on the results? Could you generalise these results to adults?

Choice number	1	2	3	4	5
Boy 1	9	11	12	14	16
Boy 2	5	9	11	15	19

If Boy 1 was in your group and Boy 2 was in the other group:

● Which choice would give maximum joint profit?

● Which choice would give maximum difference?

● Which would you choose?

IDEAS FOR GROUP / INDIVIDUAL ACTIVITIES

● This research was a *laboratory experiment*. Write a short evaluation of laboratory experiments, including comments on ecological validity and demand characteristics.

Was this the *most appropriate* method to use to investigate this research question?

The first part of this exercise is a straightforward revision of research methods. Students should be able to comment on control, sampling issues, experimenter bias as well as ecological validity and demand characteristics. The second part of this activity is more complex and, as with other activities, there is no definitive answer to this question. You could argue that demonstrating that discrimination occurs in even the most minimal of groups and 'unreal' of situations is evidence of the powerful effects of group membership. Alternatively you could justifiably argue that research conducted in such artificial conditions can tell us nothing at all about prejudice and discrimination in the real world.

● Prejudice and discrimination are difficult topics for psychologists to investigate. Suggest how each of the following methods might be used to investigate prejudice / discrimination.:

Survey / questionnaire methods
Observational methods
Experimental methods

Evaluate your suggestions.

It should be fairly straightforward for students to suggest some ways in which prejudice and discrimination might be investigated. Concentrate on evaluating their suggestions, not to be critical but to point out what a difficult area of research this is. Students often find Tajfel's study quite boring and it may be worthwhile spending some time considering alternative ways in which the research could have been done. You will probably find that students will be able to point to problems such as demand characteristics, difficulty in identifying or controlling variables and ethical problems in ideas for research that may initially appear much more interesting. They may then be able to appreciate why Tajfel chose arbitrary criteria for assigning group membership and a 'meaningless' task.

● How might prejudice / discrimination be reduced?

This is not a crucial activity as the reduction of prejudice and discrimination is not specified on the AS specification. However, it is an interesting area for discussion and one where all students should be able to contribute. If you want a slightly more formal exercise, or to give different groups of students slightly different tasks to do, you could set a series of little scenarios for them to work with: for example, one group could consider how to reduce racist name-calling in a primary school, another could consider (racist) bullying in a secondary school, and a third group could consider racial harassment in the workplace.

Most introductory texts have sections on the reduction of prejudice and discrimination, and the key points to consider are **equal status contact** and the **pursuit of common goals**.

The Psychology of individual differences
Gould

TEACHING NOTES

It is important to explain to students that this is a REVIEW article. Gould did not conduct these IQ tests but is evaluating work done nearly 100 years ago by other researchers. If you have not already discussed review articles (in relation to Deregowski) you will need to make sure that students understand this. Make sure that they refer to Yerkes's tests and findings and not Gould's.

You may wish to give a very brief introduction to the topic of intelligence although I think that students can understand this review without any background material. If you do have time for an introduction you could cover the following:

● What is intelligence?

● How is intelligence measured?

● What is IQ?

● How are IQ scores calculated?

It is a useful exercise to give students examples of contemporary IQ tests and ask them to consider exactly what is being measured (verbal skills, numerical skills, logic etc.). This could lead into a debate on whether these skills are 'native intelligence' or learned skills. If they can evaluate contemporary tests, they will have no difficulties evaluating the Alpha and Beta tests discussed in the Core Study. At the time of writing, the BBC 'Test the Nation' IQ test was still available at www.bbc.co.uk/testthenation and the BBC site also has several discussion articles relating to this mass testing project.

This Core Study is an excellent one for the development of students' evaluation skills. The information contained within Gould's review is horrifying and students often find it difficult to accept how such poor quality testing was deemed acceptable. This is a good way of introducing them to the notion that Psychology has developed much more sophisticated research methods over the last 100 years and that much research conducted in the past has methodological (and ethical) flaws that would be unacceptable today.

This study also demonstrates very clearly the difference between ethics and ethical implications. Whilst Yerkes's research was not unethical in the sense that Schachter and Singer's research or Bandura's research are considered to be, it has serious ethical implications. Many general textbooks cover this type of debate under the heading of 'socially sensitive research'. A discussion of these issues could be related to the themes of **usefulness / practical applications** as well as **ethnocentrism**.

Gould, S.J. (1982)

A nation of morons. *New Scientist* **(6 May 1982), 349–352**

This is a review of one aspect of the history of intelligence testing, still a highly controversial area of modern Psychology.

Write your own definition of the word 'intelligence'.

Can you learn to be intelligent?

IQ (intelligence quotient) tests were originally designed to identify children who were in need of extra academic help, therefore making the assumption that IQ *could* be improved. This notion was unfortunately lost as tests were translated into English and attracted interest from the USA. There, the fiercest supporters of the tests were often scientists who believed that all individual differences (intelligence, aggression, criminal behaviour etc.) were *genetic* and that society should aim selectively to breed a superior race of people. This is referred to as EUGENICS.

At the beginning of the First World War, Robert Yerkes was an American psychologist trying to establish Psychology as a science. He believed that 'mental testing' was one way to do this. He persuaded the US Army to test all recruits – giving him access to 1.75 million people.

He used *three types of test*. In the table below, give details of the people each test was designed for and a brief description of the test:

Type of test	Designed for?	Description
Army Alpha		
Army Beta		
Spoken test		

What did Yerkes mean by 'native intellectual ability'?

Look at the examples of the test questions from the article. Was Yerkes testing 'native intellectual ability'? Give reasons for your answer.

What practical problems arose during the testing?

What THREE 'facts' did Yerkes publish?

1 _____

2 _____

3 _____

Outline TWO criticisms that can be made of these 'facts'.

Describe how these 'facts' were used by politicians.

What other effects do you think these 'facts' might have had?

FACTS?

1 The average mental age of white American adults was 13 (just above the level of 'moronity').

2 European immigrants could be graded by their country of origin. The fair people of Northern and Western Europe achieved a higher mental age than the Slavs of Eastern Europe and the darker people of Southern Europe (Russian: 11.3, Italian: 11, Pole: 10.7).

3 The average mental age of black men was 10.4, considerably below the white average.

IDEAS FOR GROUP / INDIVIDUAL ACTIVITIES

● Design some questions for an IQ test that measures 'native intellectual ability'. Ask members of another group to comment on your questions.

This is a lot harder than it looks, but it's worth doing if only to illustrate the problems that exist in trying to set 'fair' intelligence test questions. If you have access to books with problem solving exercises or intelligence tests in them, you could let students look for what they think are good questions and conduct the activity that way. Alternatively, let them research on the internet. There are numerous sites devoted to intelligence testing, including the BBC's 'Test the Nation' site mentioned earlier.

● Should teachers have IQ scores for all their students? Read the summary of the research by Rosenthal and Jacobson (1966) before answering!

This study is one of the ones summarised in Banyard (*Introducing Psychological Research*) but if you do not have access to copies of this text for all your students, you could simply read them the summary below:

> Rosenthal and Jacobson (1966) investigated the psychological phenomenon referred to as the **self fulfilling prophecy**. They wanted to see if the **expectations** that teachers hold about their students will influence the achievements of those students. They administered intelligence tests to classes of children in an American elementary school. They told the teachers that the tests had identified some children as **'bloomers'**, that is, those who were expected to develop particularly rapidly over the next year, whereas in fact they had simply selected some children randomly. This created two groups of children: those for whom the teachers now had specific expectations and a control group. Eight months later the intelligence test was administered again and the two groups were compared. The children in the experimental group showed far greater increases in their scores than the control group.
>
> What does this study suggest?

This can generate a very good discussion but be warned – if you work somewhere that gives A level students ALIS scores or Target Minimum Grades, this could be a potentially explosive activity!

The overlaps here with the Core Study by Rosenhan are quite marked and you might want to look at this activity again when you are considering Rosenhan's research.

You should be aware that the research conducted by Rosenthal and Jacobson has been criticised; the tests were not standardised for the age range of children used and the results may therefore be meaningless. There is also some doubt over whether the teachers took much notice of the lists of bloomers and may not have had any expectations created.

● Will intelligence always be the same – in different cultures or at different times?

This is a more philosophical debate and so may be more appropriate if you are looking at this Core Study late in the course. It can create an excellent discussion of the nature–nurture debate and the way in which all behaviours can be understood as adaptations to the environment. However, this is not an essential debate for the students to have and you may feel that it is too demanding at this stage.

Hraba and Grant

TEACHING NOTES

Although this study is in the Psychology of individual differences section, it considers the changes to individual Psychology as a result of **changes in society**. You may have considered some of these issues already when considering whether Milgram or Haney, Banks and Zimbardo would have found the same results if they replicated their studies 30 or 40 years later.

This Core Study looks at racial awareness (racial identification and racial preference) in young black children and white children. It uses a technique of doll choice to examine the children's racial awareness and is a replication of a study conducted by Clark and Clark in 1939. You can find the original Clark and Clark study on the Classics in Psychology website.

Clark and Clark had conducted their study in Washington in 1939 when racial tensions were high and segregation still common (the children they tested went to segregated schools). They only studied black children. Hraba and Grant's study, using both black and white participants, was conducted 30 years later in 1969 when there were significantly more positive attitudes towards black people and segregation was rare. If you have time, an interesting research exercise for students would be to ask them to find out something about racial attitudes in 1930s America and 1960s America.

Hraba and Grant replicated the original study as closely as possible and asked the same eight questions. The results were then compared in two ways: black children in 1939 and 1969, and black children in 1969 compared with white children in 1969. The Core Study is a straightforward one to teach: the procedure is simple and if you have some dolls from acting out the Core Study by Baron-Cohen, Leslie and Frith you can use them again! There are quite a lot of quantitative results and it is worth making sure that students can describe these results in words without worrying about remembering all the numbers!

Ethnocentrism is a key issue to address when considering this study. Students could be asked to consider what the study tells us about ethnocentrism and to consider some of the issues surrounding the study of ethnocentrism and prejudice.

Hraba, J. and Grant, G. (1970)

Black is beautiful: a re-examination of racial preference and identification. *Journal of Personality and Social Psychology,* **16, 398–402**

This study looks at racial identification and racial preference in black and white American children. It is a *replication* (with the addition of a white comparison group) of a study conducted in 1939 by Clark and Clark.

Outline the findings of the Clark and Clark study.

What social / political changes took place between the original study and the Hraba and Grant replication?

Hraba and Grant used the same EIGHT questions as Clark and Clark. These were designed to measure:

RACIAL PREFERENCE	RACIAL AWARENESS	RACIAL SELF IDENTIFICATION

Complete the table below:

Q no	Give me the doll that:	Designed to measure?
1	'you want to play with'	
2	'is a nice doll'	
3	'looks bad'	
4	'is a nice colour'	
5	'looks like a white child'	
6	'looks like a coloured child'	
7	'looks like a Negro child'	
8	'looks like you'	

Hraba and Grant also assessed the 'behavioural consequences' of this. What information did they ask for?

Who were the subjects in Hraba and Grant's study?

Draw *bar graphs* to represent the following:

1 A comparison of the black children's results to question 1 in 1939 and 1969
2 A comparison of the black children's results to question 2 in 1939 and 1969
3 A comparison of the black children's results to question 3 in 1939 and 1969
4 A comparison of the black children's results to question 4 in 1939 and 1969

What *other differences* were there between Clark and Clark's results and Hraba and Grant's results?

How do Hraba and Grant explain their results?

Q no	Give me the doll that:	Designed to measure?
1	'you want to play with'	Racial preference
2	'is a nice doll'	Racial preference
3	'looks bad'	Racial preference
4	'is a nice colour'	Racial preference
5	'looks like a white child'	Racial awareness
6	'looks like a coloured child'	Racial awareness
7	'looks like a Negro child'	Racial awareness
8	'looks like you'	Racial self-identification

IDEAS FOR GROUP / INDIVIDUAL ACTIVITIES

● Suggest problems with using black and white dolls in these studies. Explain how you think these problems might have affected the results.

This is a relatively straightforward exercise. Students are likely to suggest the following issues: that children may choose dolls for any number of reasons; they may select the doll that has a particular colour outfit; they may choose a white doll as these are more familiar to them (and certainly would have been in 1969); boys may not want to choose dolls etc.

● Design an alternative way of testing children's racial preference and / or racial self-identification that does not use dolls!

This would make a good presentation exercise. Students could work in little groups to design their study and then could present this to the rest of the class. There are many ways in which racial preference / racial self-identification could be investigated. The best one suggested by my students recently was to look at children's favourite sports stars, singers, television personalities etc. and examine whether children tended to choose role models who were the same or different races as themselves. They also suggested asking children questions about high profile black and white personalities, such as 'How much would you like to be like this person?' and so on.

● This research suggests that the findings of psychological research have a 'shelf-life'. What implications does this have for psychological research? What other Core Studies may have a shelf-life?

This is a huge topic but quite an important one to consider. All research should be interpreted against the society in which the research was conducted. In a sense you could argue that all research is out of date almost as soon as it has been published. Specifically you could consider this question in relation to Haney, Banks and Zimbardo, Milgram and Bandura, Ross and Ross. Would the results be the same if the research was conducted now? You could argue that the BBC's 'The Experiment' suggests not, that participants are likely to be more able to disobey in an obedience paradigm (or not?) and that children may be less distressed by aggression in adults, especially women. Some of these changes may be positive ones and some are definitely negative, but the point is that all research is a product of the time at which it was conducted.

Rosenhan

TEACHING NOTES

What is abnormal? This question is a common way to introduce this study but this is a difficult concept for students to grasp. 'What is normal?' is harder still, but a worthwhile exercise which often leaves students feeling frustrated at their inability to define something seemingly so simple. If you do use this kind of introduction then it is important to follow it up with some concluding comments. I have started explaining (in very general terms) the classification systems that are currently in use for diagnosing psychiatric disorders. I explain that the system used in this country is different from the system used in the USA and that there is a different system again in use in China. This introduces the notion of cultural differences in defining abnormality. You could also explain that the classification of disorders changes with time (using examples such as unmarried mothers or homosexuality). This reinforces the notion that abnormality is not diagnosed according to some 'hard and fast' rules and that, like beauty, it is in 'the eye of the beholder'. It may be worth asking students to consider the differences between the way psychiatric disorders are diagnosed and the way that medical disorders are diagnosed. This type of introduction should at least plant the idea that this type of diagnosis is not without its problems!

You also need to consider the notion of **labelling**. How would labelling someone as 'mentally ill' differ from labelling them as 'physically ill'? You could test this as one of the data collecting activities. Try getting students to write a short account of a fictional person (perhaps applying for college, or applying for a job, or even on trial for a crime, or simply a description of a new student) and varying one piece of information. For example, a description of a person applying for a job could give details of their education and work experience. In one version you could have the sentence 'Two years ago X was diagnosed as suffering from schizophrenia and spent some time in hospital although he has had no symptoms for over a year'. In the other version the word 'schizophrenia' could be replaced with a physical disorder. These fictional people could then be rated on a number of characteristics, or their chances of getting the job could be rated. This would be appropriate for either Activity A (Questions, self reports and questionnaires) or Activity C (Comparison of two conditions). Alternatively, you could write these descriptions, photocopy equal numbers of each, shuffle them and hand them out at the beginning of this session in order to test the effects of labelling with your class. Follow this up with a short session on the symptoms of schizophrenia. (It is useful to do this so that you can explain why schizophrenia is not multiple personality disorder when you are teaching Thigpen and Cleckley!)

There are a few **methodological** issues to consider here. This is a **participant observation** as the observers were the pseudopatients but the participants were the hospital staff. There are ethical issues to consider as well.

Finally, I have never been able to understand how the pseudopatients were able simply to turn up at a hospital, say they were hearing voices and get admitted, but I suppose that might tell us more about the different health service provisions in the United States and here!

Unit 2542: Psychological investigations

WHAT DO YOU NEED TO KNOW?

The information below is a summary of what you need to know for each data collecting activity.

For each activity you should (where appropriate) be able to:

- State the research aim or hypothesis and null hypothesis

- Identify the variables

- Describe the population, the sample and the sampling method

- Describe the selection and preparation of materials

- Summarise the procedure for collecting data

- Present data using tables, visual displays and verbal summaries

- Calculate measures of central tendency and dispersion of the data

- Use inferential statistics

- Make statements of significance relating to the hypothesis.

Note that you do not have to be able to do all these for each activity. Further guidance is given in the second part of this guide.

Everything in this list can be recorded in the Practical Work Folder.

Remember – you will be tested on things that are not in your Practical Work Folder.

There are several other issues which will appear on the examination paper. You should consider all of the following points carefully – but do not record them in your folder!

- Ethical issues – both in relation to your own activities and to research generally

- Validity and reliability of your measurements

- Alternative ways of measuring the variables

- Weaknesses in the methodology and ways of reducing them

- The advantages / disadvantages of each methodology or design.

The points above MAY NOT be recorded in the practical folder.

Exam preparation

Make sure you can answer all the following questions:

ACTIVITY A

Outline the aim of your activity.

Give an example of one of your questions / self reports.

How did you select the participants for your study?

Suggest one problem with this method of selection.

Outline one of your findings.

Describe an alternative way of rating or scoring the variable that you assessed.

Identify one possible weakness in the way your questionnaire was designed or conducted and outline what you did (or could have done) to overcome it.

Suggest one improvement that could be made to the way you designed or conducted this activity.

Outline one strength of questionnaire / self report measures in psychological research.

Outline one weakness of questionnaire / self report measures in psychological research.

Outline one ethical issue that should be considered when conducting questionnaire / self report research.

If your questionnaire had been set up to investigate parents' use of corporal punishment, outline two problems that might be encountered with some of the answers.

ACTIVITY B

Outline the aim of your observation.

Describe the coding scheme (or categories) that you used for your observation.

Outline the procedure that you followed when carrying out your observation.

Outline one of your findings.

Outline one conclusion that can be drawn from your results.

Suggest an alternative way of sampling / coding the behaviour that you were observing.

What effect do you think that the above alternative would have on the validity of your results?

What is meant by inter-rater reliability?

How is inter-rater reliability measured?

Suggest how your observation could be made more reliable.

Suggest two improvements that could be made to your observation and the effects of these improvements.

Identify one ethical issue that should be considered by researchers carrying out observational research and suggest how this might be dealt with.

Outline one methodological problem that might be encountered if a researcher conducted an observational study in an unfamiliar culture.

Outline one strength and one weakness of observational methods.

A researcher wishes to observe the behaviour of children in hospital. Describe one ethical problem which the researcher might face and suggest how this might be overcome.

An observation was conducted in a men's urinal using a periscope. Why would this be considered unethical?

A researcher wishes to observe the behaviour of male and female hospital staff towards patients. Outline two categories of behaviour that could be used for such an investigation.

ACTIVITY C

State the research hypothesis for your investigation.

State the null hypothesis for your investigation.

Identify the independent and dependent variables in your investigation.

What were the two conditions of your investigation?

Describe how the dependent variable was measured.

Suggest an alternative way of measuring this variable.

Outline the procedure that you followed.

Sketch an appropriately labelled graph displaying your data.

Outline one conclusion that can be drawn from this graph.

Name the statistics test that was used to analyse your data and the results of this analysis.

Outline the conclusion that you reached in relation to your null hypothesis.

What is meant by a repeated (or related) measures design?

Outline one advantage of this design.

What design did you use for your investigation?

Give one advantage of using this design.

What is meant by an independent (or unrelated) measures design?

Evaluate the use of an independent measures design in an investigation into the effects of music on people's ability to do crosswords.

ACTIVITY D

Identify the two variables in your investigation.

Describe how one of the variables was measured.

Using an appropriately labelled scattergram, sketch the data that you collected.

Outline one conclusion that can be drawn from this scattergram.

Name the statistical test that you used to analyse your data and the results of this analysis.

Explain, in relation to the null hypothesis, the conclusion that you reached.

What is meant by a positive correlation?

If a researcher found a positive correlation between stress levels and the number of cups of coffee drunk, could they conclude that drinking coffee makes people stressed? Explain your answer.

If a researcher found a positive correlation between the amount of violent television watched and aggressive behaviour, could it be concluded that watching violent television causes aggressive behaviour? Explain your answer.

Revising the Core Studies

Students need to plan their revision around two major areas:

THE INFORMATION IN THE STUDIES

This will include the aim / hypothesis, sample, method / design, procedure, results and conclusion. They should be encouraged to produce their own short summaries of all 20 studies. I suggest to my students that they buy a pack of large index cards and write the summary on those, using the headings above. The other side of the card can be used to make notes about the themes and issues raised by each study.

THE ISSUES RAISED BY THE STUDIES

The AS specification lists a numbers of issues (themes and perspectives) that should be considered. These are:

- Application of Psychology to everyday life
- Determinism
- Ecological validity
- Ethics
- Ethnocentric bias
- Individual and situational explanations
- Nature and nurture
- Psychometrics
- Qualitative and quantitative measures
- Reductionism
- Reinforcement
- Reliability and validity
- Social control
- Usefulness of psychological research.

APPROACHES IN PSYCHOLOGY

- Cognitive
- Developmental
- Physiological
- Social
- Individual differences.

Obviously not all of these issues are relevant to all of the studies and it is important that you spend some time identifying the important ones when evaluating each study. However, it is worth making sure that you have enough time at the end of the course to revise the issues as well as the individual studies.

The worksheets / activities on the following pages will give you some ideas for how to revise these. The summary sheets have been provided to give students a quick way of checking that they can identify the aim and results of each study and the method used, with the major strengths and weaknesses. A further summary sheet has been provided which could be used for a number of revision activities (for example, ethical issues raised by the studies, the samples used in the studies, the applications of the studies and so on). I would advise photocopying these sheets onto A3 paper to give enough room to write brief notes. The first one (aims and results) is also quite useful for students to have in front of them when discussing other issues, as it will help them consider the studies as a whole rather than one at a time.

Once you have spent some time revising the studies, there are also ideas here for revising some of the issues. Tasks have been provided which encourage the students to look at ecological validity, usefulness of psychological research and nature–nurture issues. Using the same basic format, you should be able to produce a series of activities for all the other issues. There are more revision activities provided in the students' **Study Guide for OCR Psychology** published as a companion to this Teacher Resource Pack.

THE AIM OF EACH STUDY

Complete the following table.

Study	Aim of study	Main conclusions
Loftus and Palmer (eye witness testimony)		
Deregowski (perception)		
Baron-Cohen, Leslie and Frith (autism)		
Gardner and Gardner (Project Washoe)		
Samuel and Bryant (conservation)		
Bandura, Ross and Ross (imitation of aggression)		
Hodges and Tizard (social relationships)		
Freud (Little Hans)		
Schachter and Singer (emotion)		
Dement and Kleitman (dreaming)		
Sperry (split-brains)		
Raine, Buschbaum and LaCasse (murderers' brains)		
Milgram (obedience)		
Haney, Banks and Zimbardo (prison simulation)		
Piliavin, Rodin and Piliavin (Subway Samaritans)		
Tajfel (minimal groups)		
Gould (intelligence testing)		
Hraba and Grant (doll choice)		
Rosenhan (sane in insane places)		
Thigpen and Cleckley (multiple personality)		

METHODS USED AND THEIR STRENGTHS AND WEAKNESSES

Complete the following table.

Study	Method	Strength / weakness
Loftus and Palmer (eye witness testimony)		
Deregowski (perception)		
Baron-Cohen, Leslie and Frith (autism)		
Gardner and Gardner (Project Washoe)		
Samuel and Bryant (conservation)		
Bandura, Ross and Ross (imitation of aggression)		
Hodges and Tizard (social relationships)		
Freud (Little Hans)		
Schachter and Singer (emotion)		
Dement and Kleitman (dreaming)		
Sperry (split-brains)		
Raine, Buschbaum and LaCasse (murderers' brains)		
Milgram (obedience)		
Haney, Banks and Zimbardo (prison simulation)		
Piliavin, Rodin and Piliavin (Subway Samaritans)		
Tajfel (minimal groups)		
Gould (intelligence testing)		
Hraba and Grant (doll choice)		
Rosenhan (sane in insane places)		
Thigpen and Cleckley (multiple personality)		

SUGGESTED IMPROVEMENTS TO THE CASE STUDIES

Complete the following table.

Study	
Loftus and Palmer (eye witness testimony)	
Deregowski (perception)	
Baron-Cohen, Leslie and Frith (autism)	
Gardner and Gardner (Project Washoe)	
Samuel and Bryant (conservation)	
Bandura, Ross and Ross (imitation of aggression)	
Hodges and Tizard (social relationships)	
Freud (Little Hans)	
Schachter and Singer (emotion)	
Dement and Kleitman (dreaming)	
Sperry (murderers' brains)	
Raine, Buchsbaum and LaCasse (murderer's-brains)	
Milgram (obedience)	
Haney, Banks and Zimbardo (prison simulation)	
Piliavin, Rodin and Piliavin (Subway Samaritans)	
Tajfel (minimal groups)	
Gould (intelligence testing)	
Hraba and Grant (doll choice)	
Rosenhan (sane in insane places)	
Thigpen and Cleckley (multiple personality)	

Revision activities

ACTIVITY 1: 20 QUESTIONS

RESOURCES
You will need to make a set of cards with the names of the Core Studies on them. You will need one set for yourself and enough sets for one per group in your class. Your set of cards can be placed face down on a table at the front of the room or placed individually into envelopes. Students will have a set of cards face up in front of them to refer to.

METHOD
Choose a volunteer (or pair of volunteers) who will select a card from the front desk (or an envelope) and the rest of the class will have to try and guess the study by asking only **yes / no questions.**

e.g. Is it an experiment? Is it a piece of research on children?

and so on. The cards in front of them can be used to help – turn over the cards representing the studies that have been eliminated. If you do this without the students being able to refer to their notes, this will test their knowledge of the Core Studies quite effectively.

ACTIVITY 2: ECOLOGICAL VALIDITY

RESOURCES
Each group will have different coloured Post-it® notes. There will be two sheets of paper on the wall – one headed Core Studies with HIGH ecological validity and one headed Core Studies with LOW ecological validity.

METHOD
Groups will be given FIVE minutes to place Post-it® notes with the names of studies on the appropriate sheets. Each group will be encouraged to use at least six Post-it® notes (i.e. identify three studies with high ecological validity and three with low ecological validity) – it is not essential for groups to make decisions on all 20 studies! Ask groups to explain their decisions. Follow this up with the revision sheet on the following page.

Comments: whenever I have done this I have had quite different results, although I have always found that the Core Study by Haney, Banks and Zimbardo generates the most discussion and the most disagreement!

Alternatives: this type of task could be done for many of the issues identified in the specification. Try asking students to identify studies using **qualitative measures** and those using **quantitative measures**, those that take a **nature** perspective and those that take a **nurture** perspective, or those offering **individual explanations** of behaviour and those offering **situational explanations** of behaviour.

ACTIVITY 3: USEFULNESS

RESOURCES

There are a number of ways that you could do this. Either give each group 20 Post-it® notes and ask them to write the names of the 20 Core Studies on them or prepare one set of 20 Post-it® notes and share them out between the groups.

You will need some sort of continuum set up along one wall or on the board – a sheet of paper that says 'very useful' at one end and another that says 'no use at all' at the other end.

METHOD

Each group to decide where on the continuum their studies should go. Post-it® notes placed in the appropriate places. Groups are then asked to justify their decisions. You could follow this up with the revision sheet on the following pages.

Comments: if you want each group to make a decision about all 20 studies, give each group a different colour set of Post-it® notes – it makes identifying who put which Core Study where much easier!

Alternatives: this type of task could be used for several of the issues. Try 'very unethical' and 'no ethical problems', or nature–nurture to start with.

Revision activity: ecological validity

What does it mean if a piece of research is described as having HIGH ecological validity?

Give TWO examples of studies that you regard as having HIGH ecological validity and briefly explain why you have chosen them.

STUDY 1
Reason:

STUDY 2
Reason:

What does it mean if a piece of research is described as having LOW ecological validity?

Give TWO examples of studies that you regard as having LOW ecological validity and briefly explain why you have chosen them.

STUDY 1
Reason:

STUDY 2
Reason:

Choose one of the studies that you think has LOW ecological validity and suggest how researchers could investigate the same research question in a more ecologically valid way (use the back of the sheet for your answer).

Revision activity: how useful is psychological research?

Some cynics might argue that the main use of psychological research is to create work for psychologists! Other people might argue that psychological research makes a huge contribution to our understanding of human behaviour and experience and that the results of psychological research can be APPLIED to a variety of real life situations.

From the 20 core studies, choose any FOUR which you think contribute significantly to our understanding of human behaviour and / or have valuable applications in the 'real' world.

STUDY 1:
The reason I chose this study is ...

STUDY 2
The reason I chose this study is ...

STUDY 3
The reason I chose this study is ...

STUDY 4
The reason I chose this study is ...

Revision quiz

1 Name two Core Studies that are high in ecological validity.

2 Name two Core Studies that used observational methods.

3 Name two Core Studies that broke ethical guidelines.

4 Name four Core Studies that used children as participants.

5 Name two Core Studies that used students as participants.

6 Name one Core Study that offers a 'nature' explanation for aggressive behaviour and one Core Study that offers a 'nurture' explanation for aggressive behaviour.

7 Which do you think are the two most useful Core Studies and why?

8 Which do you think are the two most useless Core Studies and why?

9 Which Core Study would you most like to replicate and why?

10 Name two Core Studies that used qualitative measures.

11 Name two Core Studies that used quantitative measures.

12 Name four Core Studies that deal with the issue of ethnocentrism.

13 Name three Core Studies that used the case study approach.

14 Identify two strengths and two weaknesses of the case study approach.

15 Name two Core Studies which are review articles.

16 What is a review?

17 Identify two Core Studies which investigate the use of 'leading questions'.

18 Identify one Core Study which you think should definitely not have been conducted.

19 Name two Core Studies that are laboratory experiments.

20 Identify two strengths and two weaknesses of laboratory experiments.

THE COGNITIVE APPROACH: TEST 1 HOUR

1 LOFTUS AND PALMER (EYE WITNESS TESTIMONY)

a) What was the aim of the study by Loftus and Palmer? (2)

b) Briefly outline the procedure of this study. (2)

c) What difference did the change to the verb in the 'critical question' make? (2)

d) Comment on the ecological validity of this study. (2)

e) Who were the participants? (2)

f) Suggest TWO problems with generalising the results from this group of participants to the wider population. (2)

2 DEREGOWSKI (PERCEPTION)

a) What is a review article? (2)

b) Explain what ethnocentrism means. (2)

c) Explain what depth cues are. (2)

d) Outline the procedure used in Hudson's 'impossible trident' experiment. (2)

e) Outline the findings of the 'impossible trident' experiment. (2)

f) Are pictures 'a lingua franca for inter-cultural communication'? Explain your answer. (2)

3 BARON-COHEN, LESLIE & FRITH (AUTISM)

a) Outline the characteristics of autism. (4)

b) Explain what is meant by a 'theory of mind'. (2)

c) Briefly outline the Sally Anne task, including the questions that the researchers asked. (4)

d) What were the autistic children unable to do in the Sally Anne task? (2)

e) Why were the autistic children compared to Down's syndrome children? (2)

4 GARDNER AND GARDNER (PROJECT WASHOE)

a) Why was Washoe taught Ameslan rather than a spoken language? (2)

b) Describe TWO training methods which the Gardeners used to encourage Washoe to use sign language. (2)

c) How many signs had Washoe learned at the end of the twenty-second month? (2)

d) Which of Aitchison's characteristics of language did Washoe display? (2)

e) Which of Aitchison's characteristics of language did she not display? (2)

f) This was a case study. Outline one strength and one weakness of the case study approach. (2)

Total = 50 marks

THE DEVELOPMENTAL APPROACH: TEST 1 HOUR

1 SAMUEL AND BRYANT (CONSERVATION)

a) Why did Samuel and Bryant replicate Piaget's study? (2)

b) Outline the change that they made to Piaget's methodology. (2)

c) What effect did this change have on their results? (2)

d) How did the experimenters explain this change? (2)

e) Although the researchers are critical of Piaget, there is evidence in this study that supports Piaget. Outline this evidence. (2)

f) What ethical considerations should researchers be aware of when the participants are children? (2)

2 BANDURA, ROSS AND ROSS (IMITATION OF AGGRESSION)

a) What was the aim of the study by Bandura, Ross and Ross? (2)

b) Who were the subjects? (2)

c) Outline the procedure of the study. (2)

d) What were the THREE measures of imitation used in this study? (2)

e) What conclusions can be drawn from this study? (2)

f) Outline TWO ethical issues raised by this research. (2)

3 HODGES AND TIZARD (SOCIAL RELATIONSHIPS)

a) Hodges and Tizard's study was longitudinal. Explain what is meant by this. (2)

b) Outline one strength and one weakness of longitudinal studies. (2)

c) What were the FIVE methods of collecting data in this study? (4)

d) Outline TWO differences between the ex-institutional children and those who had not experienced institutional care. (4)

e) How did the adopted and the restored children differ? (2)

4 FREUD (LITTLE HANS)

a) How does Freud interpret Hans's fear of horses? (2)

b) Suggest one other interpretation of this fear. (2)

c) What did Freud mean by the Oedipus complex? (2)

d) Outline one piece of evidence that Freud used to support his notion of the Oedipus complex. (2)

e) How did Freud collect the data in this case? (2)

f) Outline TWO criticisms that can be made of this method of data collection. (2)

Total = 50 marks

THE SOCIAL APPROACH:

TEST 1 HOUR

1   MILGRAM (OBEDIENCE)

a) Where did Milgram conduct his study? (2)

b) What did the 'teacher' have to do? (2)

c) What proportion of the participants obeyed the experimenter? (2)

d) Milgram debriefed his participants. Outline what this debriefing consisted of. (2)

e) Suggest FOUR reasons why the 'teacher' obeyed. (4)

f) This study is widely regarded as unethical. Suggest TWO ethical concerns over this study. (2)

2   HANEY, BANKS AND ZIMBARDO (PRISON SIMULATION)

a) What was the aim of the study conducted by Haney, Banks and Zimbardo? (2)

b) Describe TWO features of the guard's uniform. (2)

c) What effect do you think this uniform had on the behaviour of the guards? (2)

d) Describe TWO features of the initiation procedure for the prisoners. (2)

e) What effect did this initiation procedure have on their behaviour? (2)

f) Briefly outline your views on the ethics of this study. (2)

3   PILIAVIN, RODIN AND PILIAVIN (SUBWAY SAMARITANS)

a) What was the aim of the study conducted by Piliavin, Rodin and Piliavin? (2)

b) What were the independent variables in this study? (2)

c) What type of method was used for this study? (2)

d) Suggest one strength and one weakness of this method. (2)

e) What is meant by 'diffusion of responsibility'? (2)

f) Why did diffusion of responsibility not occur in this study? (2)

4   TAJFEL (MINIMAL GROUPS)

a) In the study by Tajfel, what is meant by the term 'minimal groups'? (2)

b) How did the boys believe they had been allocated to groups in each part of the study? (2)

c) What were the results of the 'intergroup' choices in Study 1? (2)

d) Which of the following variables had the greatest effect on the boys' choices in Study 2: maximum joint profit, largest reward to ingroup, maximum difference? (2)

e) Suggest one problem with generalising from this sample. (2)

f) Outline one real life example of categorisation that produces ethnocentrism. (2)

Total = 50 marks

THE PHYSIOLOGICAL APPROACH: TEST 1 HOUR

1 SCHACHTER AND SINGER (EMOTION)

a) What are the TWO factors in Schachter and Singer's two-factor theory of emotion? (2)

b) What were the FOUR experimental conditions (of the injection)? (2)

c) What is meant by a 'placebo'? (2)

d) How were anger and euphoria manipulated in this study? (2)

e) How was emotion measured in this study? (2)

f) Suggest one weakness with this method of measurement. (2)

g) If an individual was given adrenaline but not told of the effects, how would you expect them to interpret their feelings? (2)

2 DEMENT AND KLEITMAN (DREAMING)

a) Outline TWO of the three research questions in this study. (2)

b) Outline the procedure used by Dement and Kleitman in their study of the relationship between REM sleep and dreaming. (2)

c) Why did the researchers use a doorbell to wake the participants? (2)

d) It is suggested that REM occurs only during dreaming. Give one piece of evidence that supports this and one piece of evidence that challenges it. (4)

e) Does a sleep laboratory have high or low ecological validity? Explain your answer. (2)

3 SPERRY (SPLIT-BRAINS)

a) What is a split-brain? (2)

b) Why had the participants undergone this operation? (2)

c) Where does information from the right visual field go? (2)

d) It is thought that the left side of the brain controls language. Give one piece of evidence that supports this. (2)

e) Give one piece of evidence that suggests that the right side of the brain may have some language capabilities. (2)

f) Suggest one problem with generalising the results of this study to people with 'normal' brains. (2)

4 RAINE, BUCHSBAUM AND LACASSE (MURDERERS' BRAINS)

a) What is a PET scan? (2)

b) Who were the participants in this study? (2)

c) The researchers found less activity in the corpus callosum of the NGRI group. With what characteristics is this low level of activity associated? (2)

d) The researchers found an imbalance of activity in the amygdala of the NGRI group. With what characteristics is this imbalance of activity associated? (2)

e) Outline TWO problems with PET scan data. (2)

f) Should the findings of this research be taken to mean that violence has a physiological cause? Explain your answer. (2)

Total = 50 marks

THE PSYCHOLOGY OF INDIVIDUAL DIFFERENCES:

TEST 1 HOUR

1   GOULD (INTELLIGENCE TESTING)

a)   Name the THREE different tests devised to test the army recruits. (2)

b)   Yerkes believed that his tests measured 'native intellectual ability'. What is meant by this term? (2)

c)   Give TWO criticisms of the tests as a measure of native intellectual ability. (2)

d)   Outline the THREE 'facts' described by Gould. (4)

e)   How did politicians in the USA use the results of these tests? (2)

2   HRABA AND GRANT (DOLL CHOICE)

a)   What was the aim of the study by Hraba and Grant? (2)

b)   Outline the procedure of this study. (2)

c)   What differences were there between the data obtained by Hraba and Grant and the data obtained by Clark and Clark? (2)

d)   How might these differences be explained? (2)

e)   Outline TWO problems with the use of dolls in this study. (4)

3   ROSENHAN (SANE IN INSANE PLACES)

a)   What was the aim of the study by Rosenhan? (2)

b)   What criteria were used to label the pseudopatients as schizophrenic? (2)

c)   How long, on average, were the pseudopatients in hospital for? (2)

d)   Give one example of the ways in which the hospital staff interpreted the behaviour of the pseudopatients. (4)

e)   What observations were made by the pseudopatients regarding interactions with hospital staff? (2)

f)   In the second part of the study, Rosenhan asked hospital staff to judge whether new admissions could be pseudopatients. What were the results of this part of the study? (2)

4   THIGPEN AND CLECKLEY (MULTIPLE PERSONALITY)

a)   Why did Eve first go to see the therapist? (2)

b)   What is meant by Multiple Personality Disorder? (2)

c)   Outline TWO pieces of evidence that suggest that the patient really did have a Multiple Personality Disorder. (4)

d)   This is a case study. Outline one strength and one weakness of the case study approach. (2)

e)   Outline one ethical issue raised by this study. (2)

Total = 50 marks.

CORE STUDIES 1   MOCK EXAM 1 HOUR

Answer all the questions.

THE COGNITIVE APPROACH

1 In the study by Loftus and Palmer (eye witness testimony), participants gave different estimates of the speed of the cars depending on how the question was asked. Suggest TWO explanations for this. (4)

2 From the study by Deregowski (perception), explain what is meant by a two-dimensional perceiver. (2)

3 a From the study by Baron-Cohen, Leslie and Frith (autism), explain what is meant by the term 'theory of mind'. (2)

  b Suggest one problem that might arise if a person did not have a theory of mind. (2)

4 Give ONE reason why Gardner and Gardner (Project Washoe) decided that sign language was an appropriate form of language to teach Washoe. (2)

THE DEVELOPMENTAL APPROACH

5 Samuel and Bryant replicated a Piagetian test for conservation but made one important change to the procedure. Describe what this change was. (2)

6 Outline one ethical issue raised by the study by Bandura, Ross and Ross into the imitation of aggressive behaviour. (2)

7 In the study by Hodges and Tizard, the psychologists found differences between the social relationships of ex-institutional children and the control group. Outline TWO of these differences. (4)

8 a From Freud's study on Little Hans, outline one piece of evidence that suggests Hans was in the Oedipal stage of development. (2)

  b Outline an alternative explanation for Hans's phobia. (2)

THE PHYSIOLOGICAL APPROACH

9 In the study by Schachter and Singer (emotion), the participants were deceived in a number of ways by the researchers. Give TWO ways in which they were deceived. (4)

10 Dement and Kleitman studied participants sleeping in a laboratory. Outline one problem with this method. (2)

11 From the study by Sperry, outline one piece of evidence that indicates that language is processed in the left hemisphere of the brain. (2)

12 In the study by Raine, Bushsbaum and La Casse (murderers' brains), participants were pleading Not Guilty by Reason of Insanity (NGRI).
  a Give TWO of the reasons for insanity that were being claimed. (2)
  b Suggest one way in which the findings from the study may be used. (2)

THE SOCIAL APPROACH

13 In the Milgram study (obedience), a high level of obedience was found. Suggest TWO reasons why the participants obeyed. (2)

14 a Describe the uniform worn by the guards in the study by Haney, Banks and Zimbardo in their study of prison life. (2)

  b Suggest one effect of wearing such a uniform. (2)

15 From the study by Tajfel, explain what is meant by the term 'ethnocentrism'. (2)

16 a Piliavin, Rodin and Piliavin's study (Subway Samaritans) refers to 'diffusion of responsibility'. What does this term mean? (2)

b What does this study suggest about diffusion of responsibility? (2)

THE PSYCHOLOGY OF INDIVIDUAL DIFFERENCES

17 Outline TWO problems that Gould identifies in his account of Yerkes's IQ testing. (4)

18 a In the study on doll choice by Hraba and Grant, the children were asked questions which were designed to measure three variables. Identify ONE of these variables. (2)

b How do the results of Hraba and Grant compare with those obtained by Clark and Clark in relation to one of these variables? (2)

19 From the study by Rosenhan (sane in insane places), give ONE example of how the label 'schizophrenic' affected how the hospital staff interpreted the pseudopatients' behaviour. (2)

20 Thigpen and Cleckley used a case study to investigate multiple personality. Give one disadvantage of the case study method. (2)

Total = 60 marks

Mark scheme for Core Studies 1 mock exam

The cognitive approach	
1 In the study by Loftus and Palmer (eye witness testimony), participants gave different estimates of the speed of the cars depending on how the question was asked. Suggest TWO explanations for this. (4)	Two explanations are: 1 That they were subject to demand characteristics / response bias 2 That the wording of the question actually changed their memory of the event. 2 marks for each explanation / 1 mark for attempt / unclear explanation.
2 From the study by Deregowski (perception), explain what is meant by a two-dimensional perceiver (2)	A two-dimensional perceiver is someone who does not perceive depth in two-dimensional pictures.
3 a From the study by Baron-Cohen, Leslie and Frith (autism), explain what is meant by the term 'theory of mind'. (2)	Theory of mind is the ability to impute thoughts and feelings to other people.
b Suggest one problem that might arise if a person did not have a theory of mind. (2)	Suggested answers: unable to recognise emotional states in others, would not be able to play, take part in many forms of social interaction etc.
4 Give ONE reason why Gardner and Gardner (Project Washoe) decided that sign language was an appropriate form of language to teach Washoe. (2)	Chimpanzees do not have the correct vocal apparatus to produce the speech sounds necessary for spoken language. Also credit: ASL is a language with grammatical structures etc.: the same as spoken language.
5 Samuel and Bryant replicated a Piagetian test for conservation but made one important change to the procedure. Describe what this change was. (2)	The inclusion of a 'one-question' condition. They replicated Piaget's conservation test but only asked the question 'are they the same?' once.
6 Outline one ethical issue raised by the study by Bandura, Ross and Ross into the imitation of aggressive behaviour. (2)	Either: Protection of the children: some were extremely distressed. Lack of parental consent: not mentioned in study. Attempt to produce aggressive behaviour in participants could also be considered unethical.
7 In the study by Hodges and Tizard, the psychologists found differences between the social relationships of ex-institutional children and the control group. Outline TWO of these differences. (4)	Any 2 from: Ex-institutional children were: more adult oriented, had difficulties with peer relationships, less likely to have a special friend, less likely to see peers as source of emotional support, more likely to be friendly to any peer rather than selecting their friends.
8 a From Freud's study on Little Hans, outline one piece of evidence that suggests Hans was in the Oedipal stage of development. (2)	Any from the following: Phobia of horses Dreams.
b Outline an alternative explanation for Hans's phobia. (2)	Saw a horse fall over in the street and was frightened.

9 In the study by Schachter and Singer (emotion), the participants were deceived in a number of ways by the researchers. Give TWO ways in which they were deceived. (4)	Deception regarding purpose of study, what the injection actually was, what the side effects would be (some participants), stooge etc.
10 Dement and Kleitman studied participants sleeping in a laboratory. Outline one problem with this method. (2)	Lack of ecological validity: sleep might be disturbed, different from at home.
11 From the study by Sperry, outline one piece of evidence that indicates that language is processed in the left hemisphere of the brain. (2)	If information went to the right hemisphere of the brain (either via left visual field or left hand), participants were not able to say what they had seen / held.
12 In the study by Raine, Buchsbaum and LaCasse (murderers' brains), participants were pleading Not Guilty of Murder by Reason of Insanity (NGRI). a Give TWO of the reasons for insanity that were being claimed. (2)	Two from: Schizophrenia, head injuries / organic brain damage, affective disorders, epilepsy, passive aggressive / paranoid personality disorder.
b Suggest one way in which the findings from the study may be used. (2)	Identification of violent offenders?
13 In the Milgram study (obedience), a high level of obedience was found. Suggest TWO reasons why the participants obeyed. (2)	Two from: Location (Yale), payment, volunteered (obligation), apparent worthy purpose of study, belief that learner had volunteered too and until twentieth shock was co-operating, novel experience, agentic state etc.
14 a Describe the uniform worn by the guards in the study by Haney, Banks and Zimbardo in their study of prison life. (2)	Two of the following: Khaki uniform, mirrored glasses, night stick.
b Suggest one effect of wearing such a uniform. (2)	De-individuating, more likely to behave aggressively if wearing a uniform associated with aggressive behaviour.
15 From the study by Tajfel, explain what is meant by the term 'ethnocentrism'. (2)	Favouring the ingroup over the outgroup.
16 a Piliavin, Rodin and Piliavin's study (Subway Samaritans) refers to 'diffusion of responsibility'. What does this term mean? (2)	The sharing out of responsibility for action: the more people that are present the less obliged we feel to do anything.
b What does this study suggest about diffusion of responsibility? (2)	It does not happen in a closed environment – because people could not easily walk past they were more obliged to help.
17 Outline TWO problems that Gould identifies in his account of Yerkes's IQ testing. (4)	Test questions were cultural knowledge, not native intelligence, test procedures were problematic: e.g. Beta test requiring use of pen and paper, men incorrectly assigned to groups, no retesting, etc.
18 a In the study on doll choice by Hraba and Grant, the children were asked questions which were designed to measure three variables. Identify ONE of these variables. (2)	One of the following: Racial preference. Racial awareness / racial knowledge. Racial self-identification.

b How do the results of Hraba and Grant compare with those obtained by Clark and Clark in relation to one of these variables? (2)	Examples include: Racial preference: Hraba and Grant found black and white children preferred dolls of their own race whereas Clark and Clark found that black children preferred white dolls. Racial awareness: similar to Clark and Clark. Racial self-identification: similar to Clark and Clark.
19 From the study by Rosenhan (sane in insane places), give ONE example of how the label 'schizophrenic' affected how the hospital staff interpreted the pseudopatients' behaviour. (2)	Examples: Taking notes interpreted as writing behaviour. Queuing for lunch interpreted as oral acquisitive syndrome.
20 Thigpen and Cleckley used a case study to investigate multiple personality. Give one disadvantage of the case study method. (2)	Cannot be generalised to others, cannot be replicated.

CORE STUDIES 2   MOCK EXAM 1 HOUR

Answer 1 question from Section A and 1 question from Section B.

SECTION A

Answer either Question 1 or Question 2.

1   Psychologists use a range of different methods in their research. The method they choose could have an effect on the results.

Choose one of the Core Studies listed below and answer the question.

> Baron-Cohen, Leslie and Frith (autism)
> Piliavin, Rodin and Piliavin (Subway Samaritans)
> Dement and Kleitman (dreaming)

a Describe the method used in your chosen study. (6)

b Using examples, give TWO advantages and TWO disadvantages of the method used in your chosen study. (12)

c Suggest how a different method could be used to investigate the same research question as your chosen study and say how you think this different method would affect the results. (8)

2   The results from a small sample of participants are often used to explain the behaviour of wider groups. This is called generalisation.

Choose one of the Core Studies below and answer the following questions.

> Loftus and Palmer (eye witness testimony)
> Sperry (split-brains)
> Deregowski (perception)

a Describe the sample used in your chosen study. (6)

b Using examples, give two strengths and two weaknesses of generalising from the sample used in your chosen study. (12)

c Suggest one other sample for your study and say how you think this might affect the results. (8)

SECTION B

Answer either Question 3 or Question 4.

3   An important issue in Psychology concerns the usefulness of psychological research. Use the Core Studies listed below to answer the following questions.

> Rosenhan (sane in insane places)
> Raine, Buchsbaum and LaCasse (murderers' brains)
> Tajfel (minimal groups)
> Haney, Banks and Zimbardo (prison simulation)

a Describe what each study tells us that is useful. (6)

b Describe FOUR problems that might be encountered by psychologists who are trying to conduct useful research. (12)

4   A number of Core Studies take a developmental approach. Use the Core Studies listed below to answer the following questions. (8)

    Samuel and Bryant (conservation)
    Bandura, Ross and Ross (imitation of aggression)
    Hodges and Tizard (social relationships)
    Freud (Little Hans)

  a   Describe what each study tells us about development. (6)
  b   Describe TWO strengths and TWO weaknesses of the developmental approach in psychological research. (12)

How to mark Core Studies 2 answers

SECTION A

Remember that in Section A questions, candidates must choose one of the listed Core Studies to write about.

a   This asks the candidate to describe sample, method etc. There are 6 marks here and the mark scheme contains three 'bands' of marks. Marks are awarded as follows:

1–2 marks for basic or rudimentary content. An answer in this band would lack detail, the candidate's expression will be poor and they will probably not use any psychological terminology.

3–4 marks for more accurate answers. An answer in this band will give most of the necessary information but there may be some detail missing or the quality of the written communication may be slightly lacking.

5–6 marks for excellent answers. Understanding is evident in answers in this band and expression and use of psychological terminology will be excellent. The mark scheme clearly states that for 6 marks 'quality of written communication must be very good'.

b   These questions always ask for two strengths and two weaknesses or four problems. The points that the candidates offer should be specific to their chosen study and should be illustrated with examples from the study. If candidates offer more than four suggestions, the best four will be credited. Each strength / weakness or problem is marked out of 3 as follows:

1 mark – identification of relevant point
2 marks – description of point with either an example from the study or some comment / evaluation
3 marks – description of point and relevant example and comment / evaluation.

c   This question will ask for an alternative method / sample / procedure etc. and for a comment on how this might affect the study. If candidates offer more than one suggestion, the best one will be credited.

For alternative:
1–2 marks for answers which simply suggest alternatives with little or no expansion. These alternatives may be only marginally relevant to the study.
3–4 marks for answers which describe a relevant alternative and demonstrate understanding.

For effect:
1–2 marks for brief answers which need developing. No analysis offered.
3–4 marks for answers which consider the effect of change / alternative in appropriate detail and include some analysis (comment / comprehension). As with part a, for full marks this answer must be clearly written and structured.

SECTION B

Remember that in Section B questions, candidates must write about all four named Core Studies.

a   This part of the question asks for a description of some aspect of the study. For each study described there is a maximum of 3 marks available. These are awarded as follows:

1 mark – identification of point but not made relevant to study.

2 marks – for description of point made relevant to study.

3 marks – for description of point made relevant to the study and some analysis ('comment with comprehension' is the phrase used in the mark scheme); for example, drawing a conclusion in relation to the question.

b   As with part b in Section A, this question will always ask for four points to be made: either four problems or two strengths and two weaknesses. However, in this section candidates are being asked about more general issues, rather than one specific study. In this answer, candidates should support their answers with examples from the four named studies only. Marks are given for four points to a maximum of 3 marks for each point.

1 mark – relevant problem / strength / weakness identified but no example or comment / evaluation.

2 marks – relevant problem / strength / weakness described and either an example or comment / evaluation.

3 marks – description of appropriate problem / strength / weakness with both example and comment / evaluation.

Alternative Core Studies 2 questions

1 Psychological studies are often carried out over a very short period of time – hours and days rather than weeks, months or years. They thus provide us with a snapshot of human behaviour and experience.

Take any one of the following core studies and answer the following questions.

Loftus and Palmer (eye witness testimony)
Bandura, Ross and Ross (imitation of aggression)
Dement and Kleitman (dreaming)

a Describe the results of your chosen study. (6)
b Give four problems of using 'snapshot' studies in psychology, using examples of psychological studies other than the one you have chosen above. (12)
c Suggest how a longitudinal approach might be used in your chosen study and say how you think this might affect the results. (8)

2 Before they collect data, psychologists must decide what type of data they wish to collect for later analysis. Basically the choice is between quantitative (using numbers) and qualitative (not using numbers). The studies listed below all used quantitative data. Choose one of these studies and answer the following questions:

Dement and Kleitman (dreaming)
Piliavin, Rodin and Piliavin (Subway Samaritans)
Baron-Cohen, Leslie and Frith (autism)

a Describe the results of your chosen study. (6)
b Give two strengths and two weaknesses of quantitative data in psychological research. (12)
c Suggest how qualitative data could have been used in your chosen study and say how you think this might affect the results. (8)

3 Very often, psychological research is carried out in response to real life events or changes in society. This is known as the context of the study.

Take any one of the following Core Studies and answer the questions.

Milgram (obedience)
Piliavin, Rodin and Piliavin (Subway Samaritans)
Hraba and Grant (doll choice)

a Outline the context against which your chosen study was carried out. (6)
b Give four problems of conducting research in relation to specific real life events. (12)
c Describe one change to your chosen study and say how you think this might affect the results. (8)

4 Psychological research is often carried out on a limited number of people. The sample that is chosen will have an effect on the results of the research.

Choose one of the Core Studies listed below and answer the following questions.

© Hodder & Stoughton 2003

Milgram (obedience)
Tajfel (minimal groups)
Haney, Banks and Zimbardo (prison simulation)

a Describe how participants were selected in your chosen study. (6)
b Using examples, give two strengths and two weaknesses of the sample used in your chosen study. (12)
c Suggest one other sample for your chosen study and say how you think this might affect the results. (8)

5 The term 'validity' refers to whether a psychological test measures what it claims to measure.

Choose one of the Core Studies listed below and answer the following questions.

Hraba and Grant (doll choice)
Gardner and Gardner (Project Washoe)
Gould (intelligence testing)

a Describe how the variables were measured in your chosen study. (6)
b Suggest four problems faced by psychologists when attempting to assess the validity of their measurements. (12)
c Outline one way in which the validity of the measurement in your chosen study could be improved and say what effect this would have on the results. (8)

SECTION B

6 Should Psychology have some use for 'ordinary' people? To what extent does Psychology apply to real life? Use the studies listed below to answer the following questions.

Sperry (split-brains)
Baron-Cohen, Leslie and Frith (autism)
Piliavin, Rodin and Piliavin (Subway Samaritans)
Loftus and Palmer (eye witness testimony)

a What does each study tell us that is applicable to real life? (12)
b Describe four problems that psychologists face when they attempt to make their research apply to real life. (12)

7 Ecological validity refers to how 'realistic' the setting of research is. Use the studies listed below to answer the following questions:

Dement and Kleitman (dreaming)
Piliavin, Rodin and Piliavin (Subway Samaritans)
Haney, Banks and Zimbardo (prison simulation)
Rosenhan (sane in insane places)

a Comment on the ecological validity of each of the studies listed above. (12)
b Describe four problems psychologists face when they try to make their research ecologically valid. (12)

8 In Psychology there is a debate about whether people's behaviour is the result of individual factors, or a result of the situation they are in. Using the studies listed below, answer the following questions.

Rosenhan (sane in insane places)
Milgram (obedience)

Haney, Banks and Zimbardo (prison simulation)
Schachter and Singer (emotions)

a Comment on the individual / situational explanations for behaviour that are raised by the listed studies. (12)

b Using examples, give four problems psychologists may have to consider when they study the effects of situations on behaviour. (12)

9 Is behaviour learned or innate? Do we have to learn how to behave, how to be aggressive, how to perceive and how to be intelligent, or are we born with these abilities?

Using the studies listed below, answer the following questions.

Gould (intelligence testing)
Raine, Buchsbaum and LaCasse (murderers' brains)
Bandura, Ross and Ross (imitation of aggression)
Deregowski (perception)

a What does each study tell us about inheritance or learning of behaviour? (12)

b Describe four difficulties faced by psychologists when they try to investigate whether behaviour is learned or innate. (12)

10 Some studies in Psychology use numbers and statistics to describe human behaviour and experience. This is referred to as quantitative data. The studies listed below all collected quantitative data. Using these studies, answer the questions which follow.

Dement and Kleitman (dreaming)
Schachter and Singer (emotion)
Tajfel (minimal groups)
Bandura, Ross and Ross (imitation of aggression)

a Describe how quantitative data was collected in each of the studies. (12)

b Describe two strengths and two weaknesses of using quantitative data to describe human behaviour and experience. (12)

11 Some studies in Psychology describe human behaviour and experience without using numbers. This is referred to as qualitative data. The studies listed below all collected qualitative data. Using these studies, answer the questions which follow.

Haney Banks and Zimbardo (prison simulation)
Thigpen and Cleckley (multiple personality)
Hodges and Tizard (social relationships)
Freud (Little Hans)

a Describe how qualitative data was collected in each of these studies. (12)

b Describe two strengths and two weaknesses of using qualitative data to describe human behaviour and experience. (12)

12 Ethnocentrism refers to the tendency to overestimate the worth of people in the same group as you and to undervalue people who are not in the same group as you. Psychology is sometimes said to be ethnocentric because it undervalues or gives less attention to the behaviour and experiences of certain groups of people. Using the studies listed below, answer the questions which follow.

Gould (intelligence testing)
Deregowski (perception)
Tajfel (minimal groups)
Hraba and Grant (doll choice)

a What do these studies tell us about the nature of ethnocentrism? (12)

b Suggest two advantages and two disadvantages of studying diverse groups of people in psychology. (12)

Alternative part b questions might include:

Describe four problems that psychologists might face in attempting to ensure that their research is not ethnocentric.

13 A number of the Core Studies describe research carried out on children. The studies listed below investigated aspects of children's behaviour and experience. Use these studies to answer the questions which follow. (12)

> Baron-Cohen, Leslie and Frith (autism)
> Bandura, Ross and Ross (imitation of aggression)
> Hraba and Grant (doll choice)
> Freud (Little Hans)

a What do each of these studies tell us about children's behaviour and experience? (12)

b Describe four problems that psychologists might face when conducting research on children. (12)

Alternative part b: describe four practical or methodological issues that psychologists should consider when conducting research on children. Describe two strengths and two weaknesses of conducting research with children.

APPROACHES (SECTION B QUESTIONS)

14 Some of the Core Studies take a cognitive approach to human behaviour and experience. This includes the processes of perception, memory, thinking, reasoning and language. The studies below are all concerned with cognitive processes.

> Loftus and Palmer (eye witness testimony)
> Deregowski (perception)
> Baron-Cohen, Leslie and Frith (autism)
> Gardner and Gardner (Project Washoe)

a What does each study tell us about cognitive processes? (12)

b Describe two strengths and two weaknesses of the cognitive approach (or describe four problems that psychologists might face when investigating cognitive processes). (12)

15 Some of the Core Studies take a developmental approach to human behaviour and experience. The developmental approach attempts to describe how we develop our thoughts, feelings and behaviour. The studies listed below are all concerned with development. Using these studies, answer the questions which follow.

> Samuel and Bryant (conservation)
> Bandura, Ross and Ross (imitation of aggression)
> Hodges and Tizard (social relationships)
> Freud (Little Hans)

a What does each study tell us about the development of thoughts, feelings or behaviour? (12)

b Describe two strengths and two weaknesses of the developmental approach. (12)

Alternative question b: describe four problems that psychologists face when they try to study development.

16 Some of the Core Studies take a physiological approach to human behaviour and experience. This approach considers how our hormones, nervous system and functions of the brain interact to determine our behaviour. Using the studies listed below, answer the following questions.

Schachter and Singer (emotions)
Dement and Kleitman (dreaming)
Sperry (split-brains)
Raine, Buchsbaum and LaCasse (murderers' brains)

a Describe what each study tells us about Physiological Psychology. (12)
b Give two strengths and two weaknesses of the physiological approach. (12)

17 Some of the Core Studies take a social approach to understanding human behaviour and experience. Social Psychology looks at how social factors such as conformity, social roles, the behaviour or presence of others and group interactions affect our behaviour. The studies below all take a social approach to the understanding of human behaviour and experience. Using these studies, answer the questions which follow.

Milgram (obedience)
Haney, Banks and Zimbardo (prison simulation)
Piliavin, Rodin and Piliavin (Subway Samaritans)
Tajfel (minimal groups)

a What do each of these studies tell us about Social Psychology? (12)
b Describe two strengths and two weaknesses of the social approach. (12)

18 Some of the Core Studies take an individual approach to human behaviour and experience. This includes individual factors such as intelligence, mental health and race and how these characteristics determine our behaviour and experiences. Using the studies below, answer the questions which follow.

Gould (intelligence testing)
Hraba and Grant (doll choice)
Rosenhan (sane in insane places)
Thigpen and Cleckley (multiple personality)

a Describe what each of the studies tells us about individual differences. (12)
b Give two strengths and two weaknesses of the individual differences approach. (12)

PSYCHOLOGICAL INVESTIGATIONS

MOCK EXAM 1 HOUR

Answer all questions.

SECTION A: QUESTIONS, SELF REPORTS AND QUESTIONNAIRES

1 Give an example of one of your questions. (2)
2 Outline two findings. (4)
3 a Suggest one improvement that could be made to the way you designed this activity. (3)
   b Suggest what effect this improvement might have on your results. (3)

SECTION B: AN OBSERVATION

4 Describe the categories or coding scheme that you used for your investigation. (4)
5 Suggest one improvement that could be made to your categories or coding scheme. (4)
6 Explain how this alternative might affect the results of your observation. (4)

SECTION C: COLLECTION OF DATA TO INVESTIGATE THE DIFFERENCE BETWEEN TWO CONDITIONS

7 a State the null hypothesis for your activity. (3)
   b Describe how your dependent variable was measured. (2)
8 Sketch an appropriate visual display of your results. (3)
9 a Outline the conclusion that you reached in relation to your null hypothesis. (3)
   b Explain how you reached this conclusion. (3)

SECTION D: A CORRELATION

10 Describe the sample that you used for your investigation. (2)
11 a Describe the sampling method that you used for your investigation. (2)
   b Outline one strength and one weakness with the sampling method. (4)
12 Suggest a different sample that could have been used for your investigation and suggest how this different sample might affect the results of the investigation. (4)

Mark scheme for psychological investigations mock exam

Section A: Questions, self reports and questionnaires	
1 Give an example of one of your questions. (2)	2 marks for complete example – including response choices / rating scale if appropriate.
2 Outline two findings. (4)	2 marks for each finding. 1 mark if finding is vague or unclear. 2 marks for a well described finding.
3a Suggest one improvement that could be made to the way you designed this activity. (3)	Answer should focus on design. 1–2 marks for suggestion which lacks detail. 3 marks for well explained suggestion.
3b Suggest what effect this improvement might have on your results. (3)	Answer should focus on results. 1–2 marks for suggestion which lacks some detail. 3 marks for an appropriate and well described effect.
Section B: An observation	
4 Describe the categories or coding scheme that you used for your investigation. (4)	1–2 marks: answer lacks detail, replication would not be possible. 3–4 marks: increasing detail given; categories are explained (operationalised) if necessary and for full marks replication would be possible.
5 Suggest one improvement that could be made to your categories or coding scheme, (4)	1–2 marks: appropriate suggestion but lacking detail. 3–4 marks: appropriate suggestion, well described and explained.
6 Explain how this alternative might affect the results of your observation. (4)	1–2 marks: appropriate suggestion but lacking detail. 3–4 marks: appropriate suggestion, well described and explained.
Section C: Collection of data to investigate the difference between two conditions	
7a State the null hypothesis for your activity. (3)	1 mark for each variable and 1 mark for correct statement (no effect / no difference).
7b Describe how your dependent variable was measured. (2)	1 mark: unclear or vague description. 2 marks: clear description of measurement.
8 Sketch an appropriate visual display of your results. (3)	Graph or table acceptable. 1–2 marks if detail missing (labels, scale etc.) or if raw data. 3 marks for appropriately labelled graph / table.

9a Outline the conclusion that you reached in relation to your null hypothesis. (3)	1 mark for accept / reject. 2 further marks for statement of conclusion.
9b Explain how you reached this conclusion. (3)	1 mark for reference to significance level / probability and 2 further marks for 2 of the following: 1 mark for name / reference to statistical testing. 1 mark for calculated value. 1 mark for critical value.

Section D: A correlation	
10 Describe the sample that you used for your investigation. (2)	1 mark: vague or unclear. 2 marks: clear description.
11a Describe the sampling method that you used for your investigation. (2)	1 mark: unclear / incomplete. 2 marks: clear description – most probably named method and source of participants.
11b Outline one strength and one weakness with the sampling method. (4)	2 marks for strength and 2 marks for weakness: 1 mark: vague or unclear. 2 marks: clear description of strength / weakness.
12 Suggest a different sample that could have been used for your investigation and suggest how this different sample might affect the results of the investigation. (4)	Different sample. 1 mark: brief or unclear suggestion. 2 marks: appropriate suggestion for alternative sample effect. 1 mark: brief or unclear suggestion. 2 marks: appropriate effect well explained.

Psychological Investigations

New teachers may be concerned about the amount of work required for this unit. Be reassured, this should **not** be interpreted as four practical reports. The aim of this unit is to give students a taste of four of the most commonly used ways of collecting / analysing data. These are questions, observations, comparing two conditions and correlation.

Some key points to bear in mind:

● Keep activities short and simple.

● There is no need to collect huge amounts of data (10 participants is generally plenty).

● Do not worry about students producing 'perfect' research – the evaluation process is a crucial part of the assessment.

● Avoid designing the activities yourself and simply using the students as participants – they will struggle to evaluate what has been done. Aim to involve students fully in the design process.

● Avoid 'ready-made' practicals: they are generally too long and are often difficult for students to evaluate.

● Focus on the strengths and weaknesses of the method used and possible improvements and their effects – not on the theoretical background to the research.

When students sit their examinations, they are allowed to take their Practical Work Folder into the exam room with them. This will contain notes on the aim, method and results of their data collecting activities. Candidates are allowed to add graphs on additional pieces of paper or computer printouts of statistical analysis. These are not necessary, however, and the best folders have short bullet point information which is easy for the student to refer to in the examination.

Students will be asked questions that are not in their folders and these will be of two types. They may be asked about **general issues** relating to psychological research (strengths and weaknesses of method, ethical issues, reliability and validity etc.) and about **issues relating to the research that they have done** (weaknesses and how to overcome them, improvements, alternative methods of measuring variables, changes to sample / procedure and the effects of these).

It is therefore important that you spend **at least as much time** considering these issues as you spend on the actual data collection.

Finally, it is possible to overlap the data collecting activities. For example, you may design a questionnaire looking at attitudes to AS study and report on general findings for Activity A. For Activity C you could compare the responses of male students and female students to one particular question. The rationale behind Unit 2542 is that students experience the different methods, and overlapping the activities in this way can often illustrate how the same topics can be investigated in a number of different ways.

A word of warning: some candidates are confused by this and may get the activities mixed up in their examination. Make sure that you explain fully the aim of each individual activity. For example, the aim of Activity A may be to investigate sixth formers' attitudes to study and the hypothesis for Activity C may be that there is a significant difference in the ratings of male and female students' liking of sixth form (two tailed).

OCR issues guidelines to centres about what kind of research is appropriate and what kind of research is not appropriate. Some of the main points to bear in mind include:

Candidates must not conduct any research which

- May cause stress, distress or embarrassment to their participants.

- Puts themselves or their participants at any kind of risk, however small this may be.

- Engages in or encourages their participants to engage in any illegal activities.

- Deceives their participants in any but the most minor ways.

- Use children under 16 as participants for experimental research.

For example, you should not attempt to manipulate negative variables such as aggression, loss of self esteem or depression. You can, however, attempt to manipulate positive variables such as smiling or helpfulness.

It would also be unacceptable to use stooges or confederates in an attempt to change a participant's behaviour. For example, if a student wanted to investigate helping behaviour it would not be appropriate for them to stage a collapse in the street to see who helps, as this might cause distress to observers. This approach does not allow you to ask the participants for their consent or to debrief them afterwards (they may have walked past) and this would breach ethical guidelines. As an alternative to this, the student could use a questionnaire method where they write two or more versions of a 'story', perhaps varying how serious the accident was or the age or sex of the victim. They could then ask different groups of people how likely they would be to help in one of those situations. Note that this could be used as the questionnaire (Activity A) or the comparison of two conditions (Activity C).

Activity A (questionnaire research) has often produced work which examiners felt breached ethical guidelines. For example, surveys on alcohol use with under-age participants, drug use, attitudes to drugs, or on sensitive issues such as depression, suicide and abortion. It would also be inappropriate to ask people to reveal (especially in front of a group of their peers) their GCSE grades or similar information. Instead people could be asked to write the information down on a piece of paper together with whatever score is to be correlated with it and hand this in anonymously. Even this may distress some candidates and it would be better to choose a less personal variable. Try correlating a student's liking of the course with a score on a quiz, for example.

Avoid using photographs, whatever their source. The guidelines state that use of photographs without permission is unethical. This rules out research such as the 'matching hypothesis' using newspaper photographs. If you have students who are determined to conduct research using photographs they will need to take the photographs themselves and request permission before they use them.

You should also avoid using complete psychometric tests: for example, those measuring intelligence or personality variables such as self-esteem. Participants may be distressed by their scores and your students may not be able to debrief them fully. It is acceptable to use parts of tests but this should be made clear to participants and they should not be led to believe that this is an accurate measure.

You have the option of January examinations for AS Psychology and if you are interested in this, then this unit would be the obvious choice. It would mean making amendments to your schemes of work to complete these activities before Christmas. I would aim to spend one week on each of these activities with perhaps another week just before the examination to ensure that candidates are prepared for the examination.

The best approach would probably be to get all your students doing the same activity at the same time and perhaps to steer them in the direction of activities: for example, so that all students are doing Activity C around the topic of memory.

Some ideas for activities are given on the following pages. There are also some ideas in the teaching notes for the Core Studies. This section of the Teacher's Resource Pack contains guidance on what is necessary for each activity, an example of a completed practical investigations folder, a worksheet for evaluating each activity and some sample questions for revision.

Activity A
Questions, self reports and questionnaires

The most popular approach to this is always attitude surveys. These could be on a range of topics such as:

- Attitudes to college / sixth form
- Attitudes to new AS subjects
- Attitudes to issues such as healthy eating or recycling behaviour
- Use of mobile phones
- Study habits
- Sleep habits.

If you decide to encourage students to develop attitude surveys, bear the following points in mind:

- Keep the survey fairly short – you do not want to be swamped with data! Even two or three questions may be enough, depending on the topic, and you can always suggest that students use the technique of 'distracter' questions and analyse only the key questions.

- Keep participant numbers low. Ten participants would be enough for this activity.

- Give feedback on draft versions – especially where there may be sensitive issues involved – but do not spend too long getting the survey perfect. Think of it as a 'pilot' study – it will be much easier for students to evaluate.

- Outline the different types of response scales: Likert scales, fixed choice, open ended etc., and the advantages and disadvantages of each. It may be worth encouraging students to use more than one type of question when designing a questionnaire.

There are many other ways of conducting this activity. Any research that involves questions or self reports is acceptable. This might include a comparison of two groups of participants or a 'story' in which a crucial variable is changed. Ideas include:

- Helping behaviour in different situations

  Students could design a series of 'scenarios' in which key variables are manipulated: for example, age, race, gender or seriousness of injury. This could be conducted as an independent measures design.

- Leading questions

  Following Loftus and Palmer, students could design their own test of the effect of leading questions, using a video clip, picture etc. as source material. For example, a picture of a large number of people could be shown and the question could be 'How many people do you think were in the crowd / group?'

Note that both of these activities compare two different conditions and so would also be suitable for Activity C.

COMPLETING THE PRACTICAL WORK FOLDER

Encourage students to keep this simple. They should identify a few key questions and summarise results relating to these questions. There is no need to do any statistical analysis on the data collected for this activity.

EVALUATING ACTIVITY A

Make sure that students can do the following:

● Suggest improvements to the questions / procedure

● Consider the possible effects of these improvements

● Consider issues of reliability and validity

● Explain the strengths and weaknesses of questionnaires in general

● Consider ethical issues related to this kind of research.

Activity B
An observation

Teachers sometimes struggle with this activity and may end up using content analysis of video material. This is not prohibited by the board but it would be better to give your students the experience of observing real behaviour. This would illustrate the practical problems inherent in observational research more clearly than being sat in front of a television set.

Again, encourage students to develop their own coding schemes / categories and do not go through too many revisions. It is important that they are able to identify where improvements might be made. Coding schemes do not need to have lots of categories – very simple ones will do.

Some observations might include:

- Use of time in common room

- Use of time in library

- Food choices in the canteen

- Playground behaviour

- Use of litter bins / recycling bins

- Behaviour on the school bus

- Crossing roads / driving behaviour / use of disabled parking spaces

- Use of mobile phones

- Gender and contribution in class.

Some centres may wish to consider taking groups of students to their local zoo to conduct observations of animal behaviour. Although only one Core Study on the AS specification relates to animal behaviour, it can still be a useful exercise. Some zoos will provide talks about primate behaviour, issues around endangered species (which could generate ideas for Activity A) or observational techniques. Some zoos will supply you with examples of observational schedules which you could modify. For example, I have taken groups of students to conduct observations of primate behaviour and we have developed simple coding schemes to investigate time budgets, grooming, handedness, facial expressions and mother–infant interactions. One student conducted a time budget observation of chimpanzees (sleeping, foraging, eating, fighting, sexual behaviour etc.) and then used the same observation schedule in the sixth form common room and concluded that (with the addition of a category for 'talking on mobile phone') there was little difference between the two!

COMPLETING THE PRACTICAL WORK FOLDER

As with Activity A, keep this simple. Make sure that students can reproduce their coding schemes if asked to in the examination and that they can describe the categories fully.

There is no need to conduct statistical analysis of this data. It is enough simply to total categories or calculate percentages.

EVALUATING ACTIVITY B

Make sure that students can do the following:

Suggest improvements to the coding scheme / procedure
Consider the possible effects of these improvements
Consider issues of reliability and validity (in particular inter-rater reliability and how to achieve this)
Explain the strengths and weaknesses of observational techniques in general
Consider ethical issues related to observational research.

Activity C
Comparison of data to investigate the difference between two conditions

This rather wordy title really illustrates the fact that this does not have to be a laboratory type experiment although this type of research is by far the most popular with most centres. It would be acceptable to conduct any kind of comparison between two groups (i.e. you can have a manipulated independent variable or a naturally occurring one such as gender or age). There are numerous possibilities here but you would be advised to keep it as simple as possible. Having more than two groups or more than one independent variable is not advisable as students will get confused in the examination. Probably the most popular topic with centres has been memory and this would generate numerous ideas including:

- Leading questions and EWT

- Question order and EWT

- Time of day and recall

- Length of time between watching event and recall

- The effectiveness of different mnemonics (imagery instructions versus no instructions)

- Recognition versus recall

- Chunking

- Effects of distraction, e.g. noise, television versus no distraction

- Effects of music on memory

- State dependent memory.

Other ideas include:

- Reaction times – compare PE students to non-PE students

- Reaction times – divide groups by numbers of hours' sleep (less than 6, more than 6, for example)

- Fans of EastEnders versus non-fans and memory for a clip

- Football fans / non-football fans – memory for football scores

- Gender differences – attitudes, scores etc.

COMPLETING THE PRACTICAL WORK FOLDER

It is important that students spend some time on this as they are often let down by inaccurate or poorly expressed information in their folders. They should have a clearly expressed (research /

alternate) hypothesis and null hypothesis. These should include both the independent and dependent variable (rather than 'Condition A will be better than Condition B'). Draw a graph summarising the data. Encourage students to go for graphs of total scores in each condition (or better still, means) rather than a bar graph with one bar representing each participant. Often they select complex graphs from computer programs and would be better drawing a simple one which can be easily reproduced in the examination. If students have collected ordinal data (which would be advisable, although there is currently nothing prohibiting the collection of nominal data), they should be encouraged to calculate mean, median, mode and range. Standard deviation is not essential, although students must conduct a statistical analysis of their data. This can be a very simple test such as the Sign test or Wilcoxon (for paired scores) or Mann Whitney (for independent scores). Ensure that students understand the relationship between calculated values, critical values and probability. Encourage students to write statements of significance explaining whether their hypothesis can be accepted or rejected and giving the reasons why.

EVALUATING ACTIVITY C

Make sure that students can do the following:

Suggest improvements to the procedure and the likely effects of these improvements
Suggest alternative ways of measuring the dependent variable (e.g. recognition rather than recall in a memory test)
Describe the strengths and weaknesses of the chosen design (independent measures versus repeated measures).

Activity D
Correlation

Correlation often confuses students and they often report correlations as causation. It is important to start by explaining that correlation is a method of data analysis rather than a method of data collection and that correlation simply means relationship.

Often the types of correlation centres used by contribute to the problems in understanding the concept (it is not unreasonable that a student might interpret a correlation between the numbers of hours spent revising and the final mark on a test as causation) and it is probably best to find ideas for activities that illustrate the nature of correlation more clearly.

You could look for correlations between two observers' ratings of some behaviour (perhaps from Activity B) and this would allow you to demonstrate the concept of inter-rater reliability. You might also look for correlations between two ratings collected in Activity A.

Other ideas include:

● Short versions of personality questionnaires, such as extraversion, correlated with own estimate, friend's estimate or with student designed questionnaires

● Number of hours of television watched and number of hours of homework done (negative correlation?)

● Rating of liking of lesson and score on wordsearch related to subjects (avoid GCSE score and test results, or IQ).

COMPLETING THE PRACTICAL WORK FOLDER

As with Activity C, spend some time constructing hypotheses for the correlation. Ensure that all students have recorded a correlational hypothesis and not a prediction of difference.

Describe how each of the variables was measured and make sure that students understand that there are two independent variables (or independent measures) rather than an independent and a dependent variable.

Draw a scattergram! This can be done on computer but it is good exercise to get students to plot scores. Students must conduct a statistical analysis of their data and this will most commonly be Spearmans rho although it is also appropriate to use Pearsons Product Moment. As with the previous activity ensure that students understand how to look up significance and how to report their conclusions.

EVALUATING ACTIVITY D

Make sure that students can do the following:

Suggest improvements to the measurement of variables / procedure
Consider the effects of these improvements
Consider alternative ways of measuring the variables
Explain the strengths and weaknesses of correlation (in particular, make sure that students understand fully that correlation is not causation).

An introduction to statistics

Whenever we carry out research in Psychology, we generate data. This data needs to be understood and interpreted. **Descriptive statistics** allow us to describe and summarise data. **Inferential statistics** allow us to make inferences and draw conclusions about our results.

DESCRIPTIVE STATISTICS

1   MEASURES OF CENTRAL TENDENCY (MEAN, MEDIAN, MODE)

The **mean** is calculated by adding all the scores together and then dividing by the number of scores. This is a useful statistic as it **takes all the scores into account** but can be **misleading** if there are one or more **extreme scores** all in the same direction.

The mean of 8 10 10 12 60 would not be a very helpful figure!

The mean of 100 101 99 102 98 100 is 100.

*The mean of 100 40 120 60 180 100 is also 100 and the **mean** in this case would not reflect the very different distribution of scores.*

The **median** is the mid point that separates the higher 50% of scores from the lower 50% of scores. The median of 2 4 6 8 19 is 6. This is a more useful measure than the mean when there are **extreme scores or a skewed distribution**. It does not, however, work well with small data sets and can be affected by any alteration of the central values. For example, if we have two sets of data:

10 12 13 14 18 19 22 22

10 12 13 14 15 19 22 22

The median would be 16 in the first case and 14.5 in the second case, despite only one value being different in the two sets of data. Note that the median would stay the same if the final value of 22 was 222!

The **mode** is the score that occurs most often. It is possible to have more than one mode. A set of data with two modes is called **bimodal**, and a set of data with more than two modes is called **multimodal**. The mode is useful where other scores may be meaningless. For example, it may make more sense to know the **most common** responses to a question rather than the mean response. This does have its limitations and when there are only a few scores representing each value, very small changes can dramatically alter the mode. For example:

3 6 8 9 10 10   mode = 10

3 3 6 8 9 10   mode = 3

However, the mode will always be a value that actually exists in your data, which may not be true of other measures of central tendency.

2   MEASURES OF VARIABILITY OR DISPERSION

The **range** is the difference between the smallest and largest number in a set of scores. It is a fairly crude measure of variability since it only takes the highest and lowest scores into account and one very high or very low score can distort the data.

The **standard deviation (SD)** is a statistical measure of dispersion. The standard deviation tells us how much, on average, scores differ from the mean score. A large SD tells us that the spread of scores is wide. A small SD tells us that all the scores are clustered together around the mean.

INFERENTIAL STATISTICS

When we carry out a psychological investigation we usually have TWO hypotheses: the **null hypothesis**, which states that the results will be due to **chance**, and the **experimental (alternate) hypothesis**, which predicts that the results are due to the **manipulation of the variable** being studied.

When we analyse data we are asking: '*Which of these hypotheses offers the best explanation for our results?*' We cannot prove one hypothesis to be correct, but we can make an intelligent guess about which one is the more likely explanation. This is called an **inference**. We want to assess the **probability that our results could be due to chance factors**. To assess this probability we use inferential statistics.

For example, if we carry out a study on the effect of an audience on reaction time, we might obtain the following results:

average time to sort a pack of playing cards into suits

with an audience 38 seconds

without an audience 34 seconds.

We need to know whether this 4-second difference in performance is due to the effect of the audience, or whether it is due to the variation caused by chance effects. Statistics tell us the probability that the NULL hypothesis could explain our results, that is, the probability that our results are due to chance. It is an **academic convention in Psychology** that we accept the NULL hypothesis as the best explanation of our results unless there is only a **5% probability** (or less) of the results being due to chance. This is written as $p < 0.05$.

If our statistical test tells us that the probability of the results being due to chance is 5% or less, then we can REJECT the NULL hypothesis and ACCEPT the EXPERIMENTAL hypothesis.

However, we have **not proved** that the audience caused an increase in reaction time. We have **inferred a causal link** and there is a possibility (5% or 1 in 20) that we are wrong and the results simply occurred by chance. In other words, we can be **95% confident** of our conclusion. Sometimes we need to be more than 95% confident. Would you take a new medicine if the doctor said she was 95% sure that it had no harmful side effects? In this case we would use a **more stringent significance level**, and only reject the null hypothesis if we are 99% confident ($p < 0.01$) or even 99.9% confident ($p < 0.001$).

Whatever statistical test you use, you will calculate a **value** that has to be interpreted using a **significance table**. There are specific significance tables for different tests. Interpreting the value will give you a level of significance, that is, a probability that the results occurred by chance.

If p < 0.05 this means that there is a 1 in 20 probability that the results occurred by chance.

If p < 0.01 this means that there is a 1 in 100 probability that the results occurred by chance.

This gives you a higher level of confidence in rejecting the null hypothesis. If $p < 0.005$ this is equal to a probability of 1 in 200 and $p < 0.001$ is equal to a probability of 1 in 1000.

Note that we can **never be 100% sure** that our results are not due to chance. It is possible that we might reject our null hypothesis and accept our experimental (alternate) hypothesis when the results were in fact simply a chance occurrence. This is termed a **Type 1 error**. If we were to accept the null hypothesis and reject the experimental (alternate) hypothesis when in fact the results were due to our experimental manipulation, this would be termed a **Type 2 error**.

The 0.05 level is commonly used in Psychology as it is thought to offer the **best balance** between the risk of making a Type 1 and Type 2 error.

Activity A: Questions, self reports and questionnaires

State the aim of this activity:

The aim of this activity was to investigate attitudes to study amongst 16–18-year-old students.

Give examples of the questions used, including any rating scales etc.

1 How much are you enjoying your AS subjects? (Rate on 1–10 scale where 1 = not at all and 10 = a lot; rate each subject individually).

subject 1:

subject 2:

subject 3:

subject 4:

2 How many hours' study do you do outside school in an average week?

3 Do you think that the total amount of work expected of you is:

too much?

about right?

not enough?

(Please circle.)

Give details of the sample that you used for your investigation:

20 students (10 male and 10 female)

Opportunity sample from 6th form common room

All aged between 16–18 years

Outline the procedure that you followed:

Students were approached and asked if they could spare 5 minutes for a survey on attitudes to study.

Those who agreed were given the questions on a piece of paper and sat in a quiet room to complete the questionnaire.

Participants were thanked / asked if they had any questions.

Summarise your findings:

The average rating for subjects was 6.5. Of the 20 people we asked, no one gave a rating lower than 4 and 18 people rated at least one of their subjects as a 10.

The average no. of hours' study in an average week was 6, although the range was from 3 to 15. Girls tended to study for longer than boys.

The modal response to question 3 was 'about right'. No one thought that there was not enough work!

Conclusions:

Most of the people asked had generally positive attitudes to AS study.

Activity B: An observation

State the aim of this activity:

The aim of this activity was to observe recycling behaviour in the college canteen.

Describe the categories of behaviour that you observed and the rating or coding system that you used:

We observed the following:

→ sex of the person

→ approximate age of the person

→ whether they placed aluminium drinks cans in the recycling bin or the litter bin or left them on the table.

e.g.

Participant number	male / female	age <20 20+	recycling bin	litter bin	table
1	M	>20	x		
2	F	20+			x
3	F	<20	x		

Details of sample:

Everyone in the college canteen between 12.00 and 1.30 on a Tuesday lunchtime in November. This was approximately 250 people.

Outline the procedure:

Four observers sat at various points in the canteen. Every time someone stood up to leave, they looked to see if they had an aluminium can. If they had, the observer recorded it.

Summarise your findings:

We observed 87 people place aluminium cans in the recycling bins, 34 people place them in the litter bins and 60 people leave them on the tables.

Of the 87 people using the recycling bins, 41 were male and 46 were female; 63 were assumed to be in the 20+ category.

Conclusions:

Older people are more likely to use recycling bins than younger people. There did not seem to be any noticeable sex differences.

Activity C: Collection of data to investigate the difference between two conditions

State the hypothesis and null hypothesis for this activity:
HYPOTHESIS PE Students will have faster reaction times than Art students.
NULL HYPOTHESIS There will be no difference between the reaction times of PE students and Art students.

Identify the variables:
IV – whether or not the participant studies PE or Art (any P studying both was excluded).
DV – reaction time measured by the 'ruler drop' test – scores in centimetres.

Describe the two conditions:
Condition A: PE students tested for reaction time by completing the ruler drop test three times (average taken).
Condition B: Art students tested as above.

Details of sample:
20 participants – 10 in each group.
Opportunity sample from common room.

Outline the design / procedure:
Independent measures: students were either PE or Art, not both.
Ps were tested one at a time in a staff office near the common room. They were tested with the ruler drop test: a ruler was held at a standard height above the p's hand. It was let go and the p had to grab it as quickly as possible. The measurement was taken as a measure of reaction time. Each p was tested three times and an average of the three scores was taken.

Name the statistical test used to analyse the data:
Mann Whitney U test

What were the results of this analysis?
N1 = 5, N2 = 5 U = 0 critical value for significance at 0.05 = 4 therefore this is significant at 0.05 (1 in 20)

Conclusions / statements of significance relating to the hypothesis:
As the calculated value of U (0) is smaller than the critical value of 4, the hypothesis can be supported and the null hypothesis rejected. PE students have faster reaction times than Art students.

Use this space to present data using tables, visual displays and verbal summaries:

	PE	Art
Mean	19.2	13
Median	19	12
Mode	–	12

You may attach a computer printout to this practical folder, or record your calculations here.

Activity D: Collection of data involving two independent measures and analysis using a test of correlation

State the hypothesis and null hypothesis for this activity:
HYPOTHESIS There will be a significant negative correlation between the rating of liking awarded to AS Psychology and the time taken to complete a Psychology-related word search. (The more they like Psychology, the quicker they will complete the word search.)
NULL HYPOTHESIS There will be no significant correlation between the rating of liking awarded to AS Psychology and the time taken to complete a Psychology-related word search.

Describe the two variables and how they were measured:
1 Rating of liking for Psychology AS: measured by rating scale where 1 = not at all and 10 = a lot (see Activity A).
2 Score on word search task: time taken to complete Psychology-related word search task – in seconds.

Details of sample:
20 students (14 female and 6 male) all studying Psychology AS.
All aged between 16–18 years old.

Summarise the procedure:
Participants were asked to rate how much they enjoyed AS Psychology (1 = not at all and 10 = a lot). When they had done this the ps were asked to participate in a further study. All agreed and were seated in a quiet room and given a word search task containing 20 Psychology words (relating to the Core Studies covered so far). Each p was timed.

Use this space to present data using tables, visual displays and verbal summaries:

Name the statistical test used to analyse your data:
Spearman's rank

What were the results of the statistical analysis?
Rho = −0.65 significant at 0.05 (1 in 20)

Conclusions / statements of significance relating to the hypothesis:
As the calculated value of rho (−0.65) is larger than the critical value of 0.56, the hypothesis can be supported and the null hypothesis rejected. There is a significant negative correlation between the rating of liking for psychology and the time taken to complete the Psychology word search.

You may attach a computer printout to this practical folder or record your calculations here.

Evaluation Sheet – not to be taken into the examination

ACTIVITY A: QUESTIONS, SELF REPORTS AND QUESTIONNAIRES

Outline TWO strengths of the questionnaire / self report method of collecting data:

1

2

Outline TWO weaknesses with the questionnaire / self report method of collecting data:

1

2

Outline ONE ethical issue that should be considered when using the questionnaire / self report method in psychological research.

What is meant by RELIABILITY?

How could you ensure that your questionnaire / self report was reliable?

What is meant by VALIDITY?

How could you ensure that your questionnaire / self report was valid?

Outline TWO improvements that could be made to your questionnaire / self report. (Hint – think about different ways of asking the questions, or alternative ways of asking people to answer, such as open-ended questions, fixed choice questions or Likert scales.

1

2

Suggest how each of the improvements outlined above would affect the results of your questionnaire / self report?

1

2

Can you think of any other improvements that could be made to this activity? (for example, the instructions you gave to participants, the environment in which people completed the questionnaire / self report etc.).

Which sampling method did you use to select your participants?

Evaluate the sampling method that you have described above.

Any other comments on this activity.

Outline TWO strengths of the observation method of collecting data:

1

2

Outline TWO weaknesses with the observation method of collecting data:

1

2

Outline ONE ethical issue that should be considered when using observational methods in psychological research.

What is meant by RELIABILITY?

How could you ensure that your observation was reliable? (Hint – how would you ensure that you had inter-rater reliablity?)

What is meant by VALIDITY?

How could you ensure that your observation was valid?

Outline TWO improvements that could be made to your observation. (Hint – if you were going to repeat the observation would you keep the same categories? Can you think of any changes to the categories or any additional categories?)

1

2

Suggest how each of the improvements outlined above would affect the results of your observation (think about reliability and validity).

1

2

Can you think of any other improvements that could be made to this activity? (For example, where you chose to observe, the length of time or the time or day, the number of participants observed etc.).

Which sampling method did you use to select your participants?

Evaluate the sampling method that you have described above.

Any other comments on this activity.

Evaluation Sheet – not to be taken into the examination

ACTIVITY C: COMPARISON OF DATA TO INVESTIGATE THE DIFFERENCE BETWEEN TWO CONDITIONS

There are a number of ways of investigating the difference between two conditions. Manipulating one variable and measuring another is EXPERIMENTAL research and this could either be conducted in the laboratory (controlled conditions) or in the 'field' (in a real-life setting). Comparisons can also be made between already existing groups such as different age groups or between the sexes, and this is termed natural or quasi-experiment.

Which of the above methods did you use?

Outline ONE STRENGTH and ONE WEAKNESS of the method that you used.

Strength:

Weakness:

You will also have had to select an experimental DESIGN. You may have used REPEATED measures where you tested the same participants in each condition or you may have used INDEPENDENT measures where you tested different people in each condition.

Which DESIGN did you use for this activity?

Outline ONE STRENGTH and ONE WEAKNESS with the design that you used.

Strength:

Weakness:

Outline ONE ethical issue that should be considered when using the experimental method in psychological research.

Suggest ONE alternative way of measuring your dependent variable. (For example, if you tested memory by asking people to 'free recall' you could suggest using a 'recognition' test instead.)

What EFFECT do you think that this alternative would have on the results of your activity?

Outline TWO improvements that could be made to your activity. (Hint – think about the procedure that you used and the conditions in which participants were tested.)

1

2

Suggest how each of the improvements outlined above would affect the results of your activity.

1

2

Which sampling method did you use to select your participants?

Evaluate the sampling method that you have described above.

Any other comments on this activity.

Correlation is a method of data analysis rather than a measure of data collection. Outline ONE STRENGTH and ONE WEAKNESS of the correlational method.

Strength:

Weakness:

In a correlational design, you measure both variables. For EACH variable, think of an alternative way that this could have been measured.

Variable 1:

Alternative

Variable 2:

Alternative

For each of the alternatives you have described above, suggest how they might affect the results of your correlation.

Alternative 1:

Alternative 2:

Outline TWO further improvements that could be made to your correlation. (Hint – think about the conditions in which participants were tested, or the instructions that they were given.)

1

2

Suggest how each of the improvements outlined above would affect the results of your correlation.

1

2

Which sampling method did you use to select your participants?

Evaluate the sampling method that you have described above.

Any other comments on this activity.